# A SECOND

# REPORT

# OF THE

# RENEWING

# CONGRESS

# PROJECT

DIRECTORS:

## THOMAS E. MANN

## NORMAN J. ORNSTEIN

JOINTLY SPONSORED BY

## THE AMERICAN ENTERPRISE INSTITUTE

## AND THE BROOKINGS INSTITUTION

# ■ PREFACE

This is the second report of the Renewing Congress Project, a joint effort of the American Enterprise Institute and The Brookings Institution designed to give an independent assessment of Congress and to offer recommendations for improving its effectiveness and restoring its legitimacy within the American political system.

Our first report, issued shortly after the 1992 elections, was designed to provide new and returning members of the House of Representatives with a perspective on congressional reform as it related to the organizing meetings of the House Democratic Caucus and the House Republican Conference. That report emphasized the need to strengthen the ability of Congress to set an agenda and act upon it, increase the quality of deliberation and debate, improve the relations between the parties, reform the campaign finance system, and clean up Congress' internal support system. A number of our specific recommendations were adopted by the House Democratic Caucus; others continue to be discussed by reform task forces in both parties.

This report is a revision and expansion of testimony presented to the Joint Committee on the Organization of Congress on February 16, 1993, and on April 20, 1993. It addresses the full agenda of the Joint Committee, including committees, floor deliberation, and staffing in both the House and Senate as well as relations between Congress and the executive, the courts, and the public. Some of the issues discussed in this report are being considered by other entities in Congress and may well be resolved before the Joint Committee presents its recommendations to the two chambers. For example, progress is being made on instituting Oxford Union—style debates in both chambers; serious discussions are also under way on reforming the campaign finance system, revising the ethics process, and bringing Congress into fuller compliance with federal laws designed to protect the rights of employees. Nonetheless, we believe the Joint Committee is the best vehicle for considering the range of problems with congressional organization and procedure, and this report speaks directly to its broad mandate.

The Renewing Congress Project will continue its work on congressional reform during 1993 and publish several additional volumes, including one on Congress, the Press, and the Public, based on a conference held May 13, 1993.

Many people have contributed to this report and to the other activities and products of the Renewing Congress Project, by participating in roundtable discussions and conferences, conducting research, writing memoranda and commissioned papers, and providing critiques of draft documents. Joseph White, Robert Katzmann, Steven Smith, and Lawrence Hansen played especially important roles in preparing the sections on the budget process, Congress and the courts, Senate floor procedure, and staff, respectively. Matt Pinkus continued his important contributions as consultant to the project; Kim Coursen and Todd Quinn provided valuable research assistance. Richard F. Fenno, Jr., Charles O. Jones, Nelson W. Polsby, Cokie Roberts, and Catherine E. Rudder serve on the Advisory Committee that provides overall guidance to the project. We are grateful to all of them.

We are especially grateful to the many members of Congress and their staff who spent hours with us discussing the problems of the institution. Many of their comments from our roundtables are used in this report to underscore our discussion and recommendations.

Financial support for the Renewing Congress Project is provided by a number of private foundations, including the Carnegie Corporation of New York, The John D. and Catherine T. MacArthur Foundation, The Ford Foundation, The John and Mary R. Markle Foundation, The Robert Wood Johnson Foundation, the John M. Olin Foundation, Inc., and The Henry Luce Foundation, Inc.

The interpretations and conclusions presented here are solely ours and should not be ascribed to the persons whose assistance is acknowledged above, to any group that funded the research reported herein, or to the trustees, officers, or other staff members of the American Enterprise Institute or The Brookings Institution.

Thomas E. Mann
Director of Governmental Studies
The Brookings Institution

Norman J. Ornstein
Resident Scholar
American Enterprise Institute

June 1993
Washington, D.C.

# ■ CONTENTS

# INTRODUCTION

For many critics of Congress, including a large segment of the public, the agenda for congressional reform is obvious: limit terms, give the president a line-item veto, pass a constitutional amendment to balance the budget, slash congressional staffs, eliminate perks, cut salaries, and outlaw the influence of special interests. The task is to cut Congress and its entrenched incumbents back to size by depriving them of the institutional and individual resources they need to pursue their parochial interests. Since Congress is populated by self-serving career politicians out of touch with ordinary Americans and inattentive to the public interest, only radical surgery can contain the cancer of political ambition and restore the health of our democratic experiment.

This profoundly cynical view of the contemporary Congress would undoubtedly shock the framers of our constitutional system, who carefully fashioned an independent and powerful legislature as the bedrock of representative democracy. But today Congress bashing is a sport enjoyed (or at least engaged in) by one and all. Network news programs and radio talk shows drip with contempt for a Congress whose penchant for scandal and scramble for pork, in the view of producers and anchors, provide ample material and transparent justification for their increasingly negative coverage. Why should news professionals be reticent about bashing Congress when many of its own members regularly denounce their institution with vitriolic rhetoric ready-made for the evening news?

Ironically, the excesses of Congress bashing may well serve the interests of those defending the status quo within the institution. The hyperbole of the broadside attack on Congress and the headline-grabbing extremism of proposals for change deflect attention from much-needed efforts to address real problems in the House and Senate, and signal influential forces inside Congress that no public reward will follow serious institutional reform. Indeed, the danger is that this round of congressional reform will be victimized by the very institutional weaknesses that should be the focus of today's reformers: being hypersensitive to public opinion, playing to the media, holding to preconceived positions without any willingness to be persuaded by new information and reasoned argument, having more concern for appearances than for outcomes, wanting to strengthen one's political position back home at the expense of the institution, cloaking personal and partisan agendas in the guise of reform.

It is not at all clear whether in this environment Congress can deliberate seriously about its own organization, procedures, and resources, and then agree to changes that offer realistic promise of improving its performance. But an essential first step is to develop an explicit view of the proper role of Congress and its place in the national political system.

What kind of Congress do we want? To begin with, it is our judgment that the best Congress is one that is strong, self-confident, and assertive. To be sure, this Congress should exist in an environment where its partner and rival institutions, the executive and the judiciary, are also strong, self-confident, and assertive. But reformers should advance institutional changes that strengthen Congress, and resist those that weaken the legislative branch.

What do we mean by strengthening Congress in this context? To begin, a stronger Congress would improve its ability to come to independent judgment on public policy issues, while allowing adequate avenues to express the full range of diverse viewpoints represented in the institution, including those of the minority party. There is, to be sure, a built-in tension here. Congress elects 535 people individually, each representing his or her own constituency. But the role of the institution and its decisionmaking structures is to transform the innate individualism and parochialism in the institution into a collective judgment. The tension between representation and policymaking must be appropriately balanced. We believe that the system of late has tilted too far toward the interests and ambitions of individual members at the expense of collective responsibility, and the balance needs redress.

A stronger Congress would give the majority the tools it needs to set an institu-tional agenda and to act on it, to express its collective voice when it can do so. And a stronger Congress would have a much improved deliberative capacity—a greater ability, in other words, to study and debate alternatives, to process and communicate information, both for considering legislation and, more broadly, for educating members and the public alike.

Our task in this report is to suggest where we believe Congress falls short of these standards and what reforms might improve its institutional capacity. Our recommendations to create more opportunities for genuine deliberation, encourage bargaining, focus attention on major, long-term problems rather than minor, short-term ones, and upgrade the professionalism within Congress are designed to strengthen its comparative advantages. In almost every case, this will entail finding an appropriate balance between features of the institution that are naturally in conflict. Congress' strength as a representative body must be balanced by its responsibility to legislate national policy. The interests and ambitions of individual members must be constrained by the needs of the institution. The necessary decentralization of the committee system must be tempered with coordinating mechanisms that ensure timely legislative action. A robust and accountable majority party must not ride roughshod over the minority.

Throughout this report, whether we are

wrestling with problems in the committee
system, the budget process, the floor, or the
staff, we will try to identify the trade-offs
necessary to achieve an acceptable (if not
always optimal) balance between the democratic critique of Congress and its republican needs. Reformers must be sensitive to
the frustrations of the public but not blinded
by them to what would actually improve and
strengthen Congress. We hope this report
will help members rise to James Madison's
challenge to "refine and enlarge public
views" and in the process renew Congress
rather than further diminish it.

# ETHICS AND THE PUBLIC REPUTATION OF CONGRESS

## PUBLIC UNDERSTANDING OF CONGRESS

Congress needs no reminder of the abysmally low level of confidence the public has in its national legislature. Indeed, growing public hostility toward Congress is largely responsible for reform being on the agenda today. Increasing the public's respect for and appreciation of Congress will require, most critically, improvements in the big picture: sustained economic growth whose benefits are enjoyed by all members of society and cooperation between the president and Congress on the major problems that we confront. The public reputation of Congress would also be enhanced by steps designed to restore its institutional integrity (campaign finance, ethics, and lobbying reform) and to strengthen its agenda-setting and deliberative capacities.

Therefore, it would be a mistake for Congress to see its crisis of legitimacy as largely a public relations problem, and design its response accordingly. On the other hand, the widespread public ignorance of Congress—the mismatch between the visceral, largely uninformed reaction of many Americans to the national legislature and its real strengths and weaknesses—is very disconcerting. The public seems to be sorely lacking in any real understanding of the constitutional responsibilities of Congress and how it does its job.

We believe that Congress can itself take several useful steps to begin to remedy this situation. Some of the recommendations we made in our first report—especially those that improve the ability of Congress to deliberate and debate—would help public understanding. But other steps are needed as well. Congressional leaders must take a more active role in informing the public and shaping opinion about their institution. Individual members must educate the public about the essential nature of a legislative body and the important trade-offs, compromises, and sacrifices that must be part of any effective lawmaking process. Instead of bashing the institution for their own political advantage back home—running for Congress by running against it—members should take seriously their responsibility to inform their constituents and strengthen their institution. Congress has been weakened in recent years by the decline in the number of its members who are committed to the institution as the bedrock of American democracy.

But no effort to increase public understanding of Congress will succeed without changes in the way the media cover Congress. A shrinking news hole for Congress and government more generally, combined with increasingly negative and scandal-based coverage of what is considered news, whets the public appetite for conspiracy theories and hardens the widespread cynicism about those who govern. Members of the press should not be expected to act as apologists for members of Congress or the institution itself, but rather as educated and informed purveyors of information. Improved coverage of Congress and the legislative process could go a long way toward bringing about some greater public understanding and, ultimately, raising the level of the public debate. Although we despair of any marked improvement in media coverage of Congress any time soon, we will explore the possibilities in a forthcoming volume entitled *Congress, the Press, and the Public.*

■ *"The truth is, the quality of the Congress is better than it was years ago, and yet people think we're a bunch of dumb scoundrels"*

**VERBATIM FROM THE ROUNDTABLES**

## ETHICS PROCESS

To large numbers of Americans, congressional ethics is an oxymoron. The focus on ethical violations, by individuals and institution-wide, including a series of highly publicized, often televised, hearings and investigations in both the House and Senate, has created that unfortunate and inaccurate public judgment. But accurate or not, the public view is important, and it is clearly influenced by the way in which Congress fulfills its constitutional mandate to judge its own members and employees.

For several decades, both the House

and Senate have used permanent committees as the primary vehicle for considering
allegations of wrongdoing or violations of
ethical standards by lawmakers. These
committees have usually consisted of hard-
working, fair-minded, and highly respected
lawmakers. But they have raised many
problems with the ethics process in Congress.

Committees that consist of current lawmakers have an innate conflict of interest
when judging their colleagues. That interest may be partisan or individual. It may
be positive or negative—that is, some may
have an interest in protecting a colleague
from serious penalty, and others in seeing a
colleague embarrassed, wounded, or removed from office. Partisan margins, positions
on committees or chairmanships, outcomes of
individual issues—all may be changed depending on whether a colleague is repri-
manded, censured, or expelled. No matter
what the outcome of an investigation, or
what recommendation is made by an ethics
panel to the full chamber, it can be clouded
by these questions—by the perception, if
not the reality, of conflict of interest. One
consequence is the deterioration of public
confidence in Congress.

At the same time, for Congress to take
away from its core policymaking tasks some
of its best and most gifted lawmakers—representing, for the Senate, a meaningful per-

centage of the whole body—means that
Congress weakens its own capacity to do its
main job. The Packwood case, now upon
us, is a good example. The next several
months will have the Senate rightfully im-
mersed in the task of dealing with the major legislative priorities of the president
and the country. To have six of its members
required to suspend much of their legislative efforts to investigate the allegations
against Senator Bob Packwood greatly
weakens the capacity of the Senate to
do its job.

It is not easy to find an appropriate alternative to the existing process. The Con-
stitution does specify that Congress should
police itself, but bringing outsiders into the
ethics process worries lawmakers, who
rightfully are sensitive about the needs and
demands of a uniquely political body. Having nonmembers judge their fates and reputations is risky.

But if change is necessary, as we believe it is, there are reasonable and appropriate ways to strike a better balance than
the current system does. In the past, we
have advocated House and Senate ethics
committees that consist of former members,
who, by virtue of some distance from the
process, do not have the same problems of
inherent conflict in judging members of
Congress as sitting members, and yet who

have a clear understanding of the unique nature of a legislature. These committees would not pass final judgment on ethics questions for Congress, but rather would investigate, hold hearings, and make recommendations to be acted on by the House or Senate as a whole.

This solution was not perfect. Finding enough former members with the time, energy, resources, and inclination to serve as full-time panelists, while avoiding any conflicts of interest among them, could prove to be nettlesome.

To deal with these problems, we have another suggestion.

**The House and Senate should each designate pools consisting of a large number of former members, along with others whose experience and background make them appropriate persons to judge ethics issues involving members of Congress and their employees. When an ethics question emerges of some sensitivity and importance about an individual, or possibly about establishing a broad policy or specific rule to govern an area of conduct where no appropriate policy exists, the Majority and Minority Leaders could each designate five members from the pool to sit as an ad hoc panel, which would then forward its recommendations to the internal ethics committees, and then, if necessary, to the House or Senate floors for consideration and votes.**

These ad hoc panels could draw on existing ethics staffs in the chambers for clerical or technical assistance. They would obviate the need for any independent counsels, whose necessity has been governed by the public and press perception of internal conflict of interest, but whose existence creates problems of its own—including the individual ambitions of the independent counsels themselves.

Few reforms would be as timely, or do as much to improve the public perception of Congress, as a constructive revision of the ethics process.

## APPLYING FEDERAL LAWS TO CONGRESS

Adding to the widespread public perception that unethical behavior is more the rule than the exception in Congress is the belief that the institution exempts itself from the same laws it expects the rest of the country to follow. Congress has customarily exempted itself on various grounds from such federal laws as Occupational Safety and Health, Fair Labor Standards, and the Freedom of Information Act, emphasizing separation-of-powers intrusions if the executive branch were allowed to enforce such laws. There are also practical questions on the relevance of certain laws, such as Freedom of Information, in the congressional context, since Congress does not execute the laws, receives correspondence from constituents that is intended to be private, and lacks a staff bureaucracy in committees and other offices to respond to requests for documents.

Nonetheless, it is obvious that the exemptions have gone too far for too long, in the process damaging the credibility of the institution itself and the laws it passes. This issue is also one of fairness for congressional employees. Staff deserve additional rights and protections if Congress is to do away with most vestiges of the "Last Plantation" mentality, which still persists today. The constitutional arguments have become an excuse to deny protection to personnel who work on Capitol Hill. Within the constraints of the separation of powers, there are ways for Congress to address this issue in a manner that provides real reform and protections for its personnel.

**We believe Congress should create an independent agency within the legislative branch, subsuming the existing entities in the Senate and House established to police fair employment practices, that would be charged with ensuring that Congress applies to itself comparable rules and penalties for laws it writes for others. Current lawmakers should have minimal direct involvement in the agency. This new Office of Congressional Compliance should first be charged with reporting on the applicability of all appropriate laws to Congress and recommending necessary changes in statutes to bring Congress into line with public expectations.**

## CAMPAIGN FINANCE

Finally, no effort to deal with the ethical concerns about Congress, or to revitalize its deliberative and policymaking capabilities, can possibly succeed without a major overhaul of the campaign finance system. In our initial report we laid out a critique of the present system (the money chase, excessive reliance on "interested" money, and the competitive disadvantage of challengers) and principles and guidelines for crafting a new system. To underscore the inextricable link between campaign finance reform and rebuilding public confidence in Congress, we repeat those principles and guidelines here.

- The primary objective is not to reduce the overall amount of money raised and spent on congressional campaigns but rather to distribute it more equitably among incumbents and challengers. The problem is not too much communication but one-sided communication.

■ The mix of contributions to congressional campaigns should be altered to increase the weight of small individual contributors and decrease the amount of special-interest money.

■ Public funding must be an essential element of an improved system, whether through tax credits, free or subsidized mailings, vouchers for radio and television advertisements, or grants or matching funds for qualifying candidates.

■ The cost of campaigns should be constrained by requiring television and radio stations to provide the lowest cost commercial rates for political ads by qualified congressional candidates.

■ If spending limits are to be included in a reform package, they should be set at a relatively high level (above the amount needed by a challenger to wage a visible campaign) and indexed to inflation. Spending limits are acceptable only in the context of generous public subsidies to candidates.

■ Soft money contributions from individuals, corporations, unions, and foreign nationals—contributions to political parties not regulated by federal election laws—should be limited in size and more fully disclosed. Political parties must be strengthened, but not by encouraging them to cater to wealthy individuals and powerful interests.

■ Timely and accurate public disclosure is essential to a healthy campaign finance system. The Federal Election Commission should be strengthened organizationally and financially.

As we noted in our first report, identifying the problems with the campaign finance system is infinitely easier than fashioning an effective and acceptable solution to them. We do not pretend that

the direction of reform is obvious or
that the route is politically easy. Reasonable people disagree about means and
ends when it comes to the financing of
elections. But we are convinced that
constructive campaign finance reform
is not only possible but absolutely essential to strengthening the Congress and
restoring the institution's legitimacy
with the people.

THE COMMITTEE SYSTEM

Nearly twenty years ago, the Bolling Committee, issuing its report to the House of Representatives to accompany its draft reform resolution, listed eight objectives that guided its work.

■ The jurisdictional responsibilities of House committees should be thoroughly modernized.

■ The House should be organized to give coherent consideration to broad, pressing national problems.

■ The House should take steps to limit committee assignments.

■ Committee jurisdictions should be equalized to afford each member of the House an opportunity to participate meaningfully in decisions affecting the lives of his or her constituents.

■ As creatures of the House, committees should be able to attract a broadly representative membership and embrace a variety of viewpoints on the questions within their jurisdiction.

■ Concrete incentives for legislative oversight should be provided, along with workable mechanisms for building upon these incentives.

■ The House should take immediate steps to develop greater coordination and more professional management for its information resources, supporting services, and physical planning.

■ The House should implement a procedure to ensure continuous review of jurisdictional assignments and encourage cooperation among committees dealing with related matters.

It's déjà vu all over again. Indeed, we can go back much further than 1973–74. If one reads virtually any report from a reform panel in the past five decades, the objectives are almost identical. The values that lawmakers and outside observers have expressed as they evaluate the congressional committee system and consider recommendations for reform have not changed. And, sad to say, the driving need they express for reforms to realize those values seems not to have flagged over the years either.

We share those values as well. In this section, we outline our own sense of what a committee system should mean for Congress and try to provide a framework to use in committee system reform and reorganization. We also offer some specific recommendations regarding committee and subcommittee numbers, sizes, assignments, and jurisdictions, as well as committee procedures and committee staffs.

We do not, however, provide a detailed blueprint for the allocation of specific jurisdictions, committee by committee. Should Congress decide to opt for a wholesale overhaul of all jurisdictions, blueprints already exist, from the Bolling and Stevenson Committees, that could easily be adapted to contemporary circumstances and issues.

We believe that some significant changes are in order, many coming from the consolidation resulting from a reduction in the number of committees. But we also believe that jurisdictional realignment is only one of many goals for the committee system, much less for congressional reform as a whole. There is no perfect jurisdictional approach that hermetically seals important policy areas in separate committees; overlap is inevitable. The Joint Committee on the Organization of Congress should not shrink from recommending jurisdictional shifts where they are compelling and appropriate. But it should be careful not to bank its entire package on a massive and controversial committee reform that itself would alter power relationships in Congress more than it would focus policy agendas or improve outcomes.

In our view, the most compelling change required in the committee system is to cut sharply the number of committee and subcommittee slots and the number of member assignments. Nothing would do more to

reduce fragmentation in Congress and improve the institution's deliberative capacity. Congress would also be well served by strengthening mechanisms for coordinating major policy issues whose jurisdiction is spread across several committees.

## PURPOSES

Why even have committees? Many legislatures do not. Parliaments have tended until recently not to have a committee system, certainly not anything meaningful. For a legislature that has no real power, where the agenda-setting and substantive decisions are made by a small elite, division of labor is not very important.

Congress is different. As a legislature with more individual and collective responsibilities than any other in history, Congress from its earliest days needed a sophisticated form of division of labor. Permanent standing committees followed soon, and the committee system quickly became the essential organizational feature of the policymaking process. By 1885, when Woodrow Wilson wrote his famous observation, "Congress on the floor is Congress on public exhibition; Congress in committee is Congress at work," it was already common knowledge.

As the basic structure for a division of labor, the committee system serves several functions for the institution. It allows for simultaneous consideration of many important substantive matters without having to use shortcuts because of a lack of time. It allows the institution to process legislation even as it brings other issues, not ripe for legislating, into the policy stream to be incubated, permitting the deliberative process to work. It allows multiple points of access for interests and individuals in society to approach Congress with their concerns. It enables Congress to legislate, investigate, and oversee executive behavior across the range-of-issue areas and executive branch agencies and departments. It creates a means for the development of in-depth knowledge and expertise. And, by structuring committees and creating centers of jurisdiction, Congress can set priorities and indicate areas of greater or lesser importance.

For individual members, the committee system defines careers inside Congress. It provides a means to utilize their talents and interests, a vehicle for career advancement, and a way to channel their energies into useful legislative pursuits, even as they develop specialized interests and expertise.

Tinkering with the committee system is thus serious business; it means shaping what the institution does and altering the most basic elements of the lives of legislators. That underscores the need to step back and define what it is we want Congress to do, and then work through how the committee system can contribute to those goals.

We come back here to the overall framework we provided in our first report. Congress needs to be able to set an agenda and to act on it. Congress needs to deliber-

ate, thinking through policy options and integrating public demands, views, and needs as articulated by individuals and interested groups into something broader, a collective judgment that enlarges upon those views.

If an overall agenda—a roadmap of priorities for a year or a Congress—can be set by party leaders and rank-and-file members, subject to events and the competing views of the president or the public, it is up to committees to define issues that might fit on that agenda and then to carry out the plans, through hearings and markups, to implement it. Jurisdictional alignments are critical here—if an important priority is too fragmented, or gets no attention at all, it will be ignored or delayed—but are only one element.

Committees are also critical to the deliberative process. Integrating public viewpoints has to come through the committee system. No substantial give-and-take on the myriad of issues in a modern society can occur with any depth outside a committee and subcommittee system. Genuine deliberation requires expertise—substantive, technical, and political—which the committee system can provide. Real deliberation requires time and attention to detail, which can come only through a meaningful division of labor.

Many years ago, committees in Congress were defined as "little legislatures." No committee system can serve its institution over the long run if its panels are unrepresentative of the institution as a whole.

For the expertise and judgment of members of committees to be heeded, the broader membership must view their efforts as fair-minded, legitimate, and close to what it would have come up with if it had been assigned to the job. Committees that are seen as too close to the interests or issues they oversee, as out of balance ideologically or regionally, will have less importance and less clout in the institution as a whole; their policy areas may suffer, and their recommendations may be rejected by the full House and Senate.

Reforms must be especially sensitive to these goals for Congress. When we look at changes in the committee system, we must ask whether they improve Congress' capacity to deliberate; whether they improve Congress' ability to identify and highlight important problems in society and to oversee the performance of other institutions, including the executive; whether they are able to act on Congress' agenda with competence, representativeness, and appropriate dispatch.

**We believe that four major elements should guide committee reform. First, the sizes of committees, the total number of slots for committees and subcommittees, and the assignments held by each member should be reduced. Second, the number of committees should be reduced, and committee jurisdictions consolidated and partially realigned to highlight important emerging policy areas and to create a better balance in the workload and attractiveness among standing committees. Third, coordinating mechanisms to deal with pressing national policy problems that inherently cut across committee boundaries should be strengthened. Fourth, new committee procedures should be devised to increase attendance, to improve the quality of information gathering and deliberation, and to strike an appropriate balance between majority and minority rights and responsibilities. As part of that effort, the allocation of staff resources among and within committees should be improved.**

## COMMITTEE SIZES AND ASSIGNMENTS

Over the past twenty-three years, we have watched Congress up close, from the inside and the outside. The ballooning number of committee assignments of members, leading to increasing conflicts in scheduling, a frenetic pace of legislative life, and a shorter attention span for members, accompanied by decreasing attendance at committee and subcommittee meetings and hearings and less real focus on important problems, has been one of the clearest and deepest problems we have seen emerge and grow.

One way to deal with too many assignments and too many committee slots is to reduce the number of committees. Later in the report, we have specific suggestions for cutting the number of committees in both the House and Senate. While cutting the number of committees will have many benefits, including some immediate effect on the slots members fill on committees, its long-term effect on committee sizes and assignments may in fact be just the opposite. Reducing the number of committees, in the absence of other changes, will lead to great pressure to increase the size of the remaining committees to accommodate members' desires and needs and to give party leaders chits to hand out as rewards or incentives.

As we noted earlier, this process has led to sharp and continuous inflation in the size of committees and the number of slots members fill. Consider, as one example, the figures in table 1, showing changes in the twenty-two House standing committee sizes over the past ten years.

Seventeen committees show increases averaging 17 percent. Three committees stayed the same, and only two decreased, by a combined total of two assignments. Remember that the size of the House did not change at all during this time. (Delegates and the Resident Commissioner for Puerto Rico are not included in the figures.) This is not simply a phenomenon of the 1980s. The increase from 1953, when the majority Republicans repealed the one committee assignment limitation created in 1946, to 1993 is even more striking: the total number of assignments rose from 516 to 857, an increase of 66 percent!

## TABLE 1. HOUSE STANDING COMMITTEE SIZES, 1983 AND 1993

| Committee | 1983 | 1993 | Percent change |
|---|---|---|---|
| Agriculture | 41 | 45 | +10 |
| Appropriations | 57 | 60 | +5 |
| Armed Services | 44 | 55 | +25 |
| Banking | 46 | 51 | +11 |
| Budget | 31 | 43 | +39 |
| District | 11 | 11 | None |
| Education and Labor | 31 | 39 | +26 |
| Energy and Commerce | 42 | 44 | +5 |
| Foreign Affairs | 37 | 44 | +19 |
| Government Operations | 39 | 42 | +8 |
| House Administration | 19 | 19 | None |
| Judiciary | 31 | 35 | +13 |
| Merchant Marine | 39 | 46 | +18 |
| Natural Resources | 40 | 39 | –3 |
| Post Office | 24 | 23 | –4 |
| Public Works | 48 | 61 | +27 |
| Rules | 13 | 13 | None |
| Science and Technology | 41 | 55 | +34 |
| Small Business | 41 | 45 | +10 |
| Standards | 12 | 14 | +17 |
| Veterans Affairs | 33 | 35 | +6 |
| Ways and Means | 35 | 38 | +9 |

Putting the figures a different way, the overall number of seats on House committees and subcommittees grew from 2,511 in 1982 to 3,177 in 1992, and the average number of member assignments grew during this same period from 5.7 to 7.2. In the Senate, despite serious restraint in assignments and committee sizes, senators still average more than 11 committee and subcommittee assignments— an amount that is unacceptably high.

The Senate example shows how vexing

the problem is. The Stevenson Committee put serious limitations on committee and subcommittee assignments for members—two major committees, one minor committee, and two subcommittees each on the major panels and one on the minor, for a maximum of eight assignments. But from the day after S. Res. 4 passed, exceptions and waivers began to appear, reaching more than forty senators—including most of the members of the Stevenson Committee itself—within a year. When the Quayle Committee considered problems in the Senate Committee system five years later, it concluded that the best thing the Senate could do would be to enforce its own assignment limitation rules. That modest proposal was evidently not modest enough; nothing happened.

Assignment inflation is a serious problem for Congress. Larger committees have more difficulty deliberating; they spend more time managing bodies and internal conflicts. Committee hearings lose any pretense of real discussion and give-and-take when they drag on to give each committee member only five minutes to ask questions. More committee members mean pressure for more and larger subcommittees, pushing the problem to the next level. As committees grow in size, chairmen have increasing difficulty finding consensus and moving from discussion to action. And larger committees and subcommittees mean more and more member assignments, which in turn mean more schedule conflicts, less attention to detail, and less in-depth work on the part of members.

**We believe that Congress should adopt tough limitations on assignments for members in both houses—written into the rules of the chambers. We would prefer that members be allowed to serve on no more than two committees (one if exclusive) and four subcommittees in the House, and no more than two major committees, one minor committee, and four subcommittees in the Senate, with exceptions only for the ethics committee and temporary investigative panels. Other exceptions and temporary assignments must end. Committees, except for Appropriations, should be limited to no more than six subcommittees, with no more than four for any non-major panels that remain in existence. But obviously, the recommendation will be empty, even if implemented, without more serious steps to put teeth into assignment limitations that are written into the rules.**

We suggest several ways to make the limitations more meaningful. First, committees should be required to report their subcommittee structure and assignments when reporting their rules to the House or Senate. Points of order could then be made against assignments or numbers in violation of the limits. Second, committee sizes should be set in the House rules as they are in the Senate and were in the House until 1975. In current House practice, there is no limit,

*■ "Ask me real quickly to name the nine subcommittees that I am on, and who the other members are. There is no way I can tell you the other members in half the subcommittees. Half of them don't even meet, but they have staff."*

**VERBATIM FROM THE ROUNDTABLES**

and the party caucus may add members for pro forma floor ratification, without limitation unless the other party wishes to require a floor vote.

We propose that initial committee assignments to fill a committee's set size be made by the respective party committees as privileged under the rules; but any assignments in violation of the fixed size would not be privileged and could be made only by unanimous consent, suspension of the rules, or a rules change increasing a committee's size. We recognize that this change would not have a huge effect, since most increases in committee size are done through collusion by both parties and their leaders. But at least the size increases would be publicly aired, and the potential would be there for a member to raise an objection.

**We would like to see another, tougher change for both houses—namely, that the rules include an overall cap on the number of slots available for committees and subcommittees.**

If the Senate assignment limits, for example, were indeed two major and one minor committee per senator, along with four subcommittees, this would mean that if every senator filled his or her allotment, there would be 700 slots occupied. Additional leeway would be needed, of course, for ethics or any temporary panels, along with a small amount of slack to meet party-ratio needs.

When party leaders meet before a Congress to negotiate committee ratios, the first agreement would come on the ratio of overall slots, followed by ratios for each committee. Then, when each party's committee on committees meets to make assignments, the slots available to each committee, including subcommittee slots, would be allocated. If the chamber exceeded the cap, then challenges could be raised when the chamber considered committee assignments and chairmanships, or considered committee authorizations or funding resolutions.

This proposal, to be sure, would be difficult to implement or enforce. But it, and others like it, are necessary to put some roadblocks in front of a process that inexorably adds to Congress' fragmentation and decentralization.

If Congress takes serious steps to cut the number of panels, assignments, and slots, it must be even more sensitive to providing an equitable distribution of power and responsibilities in the institution. We favor limits built into the chambers' rules on the number of chairmanships an individual can hold, including, for the House, limiting members to no more than one subcommittee chair or ranking membership; prohibiting chairs or ranking members of full committees from chairing or ranking on a subcommittee of another committee; requiring members serving on the Intelligence Committee to take leaves of absence from another committee, allowing them to retain their seniority rights; and counting subcommittee assignments on Intelligence against each member's total allotment.

Some, including freshman Democrats of the 103d Congress, have also recommended that full committee chairs be barred from chairing a subcommittee on the committee they chair. We believe this proposal goes too far. A case must be made that holding both a full committee and a subcommittee chairmanship on the same committee results in an excessive concentration of authority that is unfair to the committee's other majority members or destructive to the committee's success in fashioning policy within its jurisdiction. We believe that a chairman's potential dual role has been shown to be valuable in many cases and should not be casually cast aside.

There is a fine line between beneficial division of labor in Congress and destructive fragmentation of attention, resources, and responsibilities. In our judgment, Congress crossed that line some time ago, and every attempt to pull it back, even where successful, has been short-lived. Part of the problem is simple human nature. If committees, and assignments to them, are valuable commodities, the inclination to give people what they want, through more committees, larger committees, more assignments, and more chairmanships, is almost irresistible.

It is absolutely critical, in our judgment, that Congress cut back on committee sizes and assignments. Once it has done so, it is just as critical to find ways to resist the nearly irresistible, to keep the problem from reemerging immediately.

## COMMITTEE NUMBERS

It may not be obvious why larger committees, more committees, and more assignments for members are deleterious to Congress. But there are good reasons why every reform effort since 1946 has strived to cut the number of committees and subcommittees, why most chairmen have tried to reduce, not increase, the sizes of their panels in recent years, and why one would be hard pressed to find a member of Congress who is content with his or her workload or array of responsibilities.

The goal here is to meet Congress' responsibilities. There may not be an optimal number of committees, but we believe there are too many now. Too many committees mean more difficulty setting priorities (especially if every committee believes its priorities are the most important ones), more difficulty scheduling committee and floor action, too much fragmentation of policy responsibilities and power bases, too many demands for multiple assignments.

If there are too many, it does not automatically follow that the deeper the cut in committee numbers the better. Radical cutbacks would reduce Congress' ability to identify nascent policy problems, reduce innovation, and stifle individual talents. But reducing the numbers, not radically but prudently, would mean that Congress could

focus its attention more sharply on things that matter without decreasing its ability to innovate and reach out; permit a modest recentralization of authority and initiative; focus attention on which policy areas should be consolidated or highlighted; and make it easier to create panels roughly equivalent in workload, responsibilities, and attractiveness.

How do you cut the number of committees?

**First, the Senate should follow the lead of the House and eliminate select and special committees (excluding intelligence and ethics).**

The *concept* of select committees should not be abandoned by Congress; the ability to focus on a new, emerging and important policy area, whether it be hunger, narcotics control, or families, or to investigate allegations of wrongdoing, from Watergate to Iran-contra, is important for the institution. But select committees are, and should be, created for a limited and finite amount of time, to investigate, hold hearings, issue reports, and spotlight a problem. If it has legs, and can meet the tests of importance and priority, a subject or issue should then be the focus of a subcommittee on a standing committee or a standing committee itself. It is symbolic of the larger problem of self-indulgence and committee system inflation that select committees are invariably created for one Congress and inevitably continue for many more.

The Select Committee on Indian Affairs

is a good example—one for which we have special insight, since Norman Ornstein, as a staff member of the Stevenson Committee, worked directly on it. The Indian Affairs Committee was created out of the Stevenson Committee reforms in 1976-77, to deal with a specific problem. A federal commission on Indian affairs was scheduled to release a wide-ranging report the following year; at the request of then-Senator James Abourezk, the Stevenson Committee deferred for one Congress its judgment to put Indian Affairs jurisdiction in the Labor and Human Resources or the Energy and Natural Resources Committees, to enable a temporary select panel to consider the commission report. Its creation was accompanied by the solemn promise of Senator Abourezk that it would last for one Congress—and no more. It is bemusing, in a way, sixteen years later, to see the ploy to remove "select" from the committee's name as a way to avoid its elimination—since it should be exhibit A in why the system has gone out of control.

Select committees mean more panels, more assignments, more fragmentation, more staff, and less focus for the standing committees that have legislative jurisdiction. They are not the only committees that should be consolidated with other, larger panels to create some disciplined focus in broad-based standing committees with significant workloads and jurisdictions.

**Small and narrow standing committees, whenever possible or feasible, should be merged into larger and broader committees, to give them more range, breadth, and attractiveness to members, enabling them to be more representative and to have more effective means to set substantive priorities.**

We recommend first that the House follow the lead of the Senate here. In 1977 the Senate put the jurisdictions of the Post Office and Civil Service and District of Columbia Committees into the Government Operations Committee, turning it into a broader Governmental Affairs Committee, which in turn became a more important, prestigious, and representative committee than the one it replaced. The House should do the same.

Both houses should adopt a broader principle to consolidate committees further. The appropriate focus for congressional committees is substantive areas of policy. When committees have client groups as their focus, they tend to be narrower and less representative of the institution as a whole and to be advocates for their client groups. If that is not universally true—House Merchant Marine and Fisheries, for example, has been a much more wide-ranging panel under Chairman Gerry Studds than it was under his predecessors—it remains largely true of the membership of the panels, as a natural artifact of areas of interest and group dynamics.

We recommend that the House Committees on Small Business, Merchant Ma-

■ *"I think we'd be a whole
lot better off if the importance of committees were
more leveled off.  They
can't all be exactly alike.  I
mean, if you're going to
have an Energy and
Commerce and a Ways and
Means and Appropriations,
they're somewhat more
powerful.  But we've got
some committees that don't
mean a goddamned thing."*

**VERBATIM FROM THE ROUNDTABLES**

rine and Fisheries, and Veterans Affairs, and the Senate Committees on Small Business and Veterans Affairs, be consolidated into broader committees with compatible jurisdiction.  The small-business jurisdiction could go to both chambers' banking committees, which have their own client group focus and need broader areas of responsibility.  Merchant Marine and Fisheries could be consolidated with the House Natural Resources Committee and the Public Works and Transportation Committee.  The veterans' jurisdiction belongs with the Armed Services panels.

In each case, we recommend that provisions be made for chairmen and ranking members of the smaller panels to be offered slots on the new, larger panels, with seniority rights to be determined by the respective party caucuses—the example of the Senate with Post Office, D.C., and Governmental Affairs would be instructive.

These changes would still leave some narrow committees in place, including House Administration and, for both houses, the ethics and intelligence panels.  We believe that something should be done with House Administration—but we are not sure what.  One possibility is to split the responsibilities of House Administration among the Rules Committee (making it parallel to the Senate Rules and Administration Committee), or the Judiciary Committee, and the Director of Non-Legislative and Financial Services.  Another is to retain the committee but to make it a panel with rotating membership with an eight-year limit, in order to expose more members to its subject matter and to discourage empire building by a cadre of permanent members in a position to grant or withhold favors from colleagues.

As we discussed earlier, we believe Congress should retain its internal ethics committees, but supplement them for specific investigations with panels drawn from a designated pool of outside, knowledgeable people, including especially former members. Intelligence is a special case, where having a broad range of members exposed to the intelligence process and intelligence community is useful for Congress, the executive, and the foreign-policymaking process. As a consequence, we do not support creation of a Joint Committee on Intelligence but instead favor the two panels as they now exist. However, we do recommend two changes in the intelligence committees. Congress should create a joint staff of permanent professionals, patterned on the Joint Tax Committee model, to supplant the larger number of staffers on the House and Senate committees, many of whom in the Senate are designated for individual members.

Both chambers currently rotate membership on the intelligence panels, with House members serving for six years and senators for eight. We recommend that the House increase its service limit to eight years, and make appointments in such a way that the chairman can serve for at least

four years, as previously recommended by Representative Lee Hamilton, a former chairman of the Intelligence Committee.

Members of the House Budget Committee rotate after six years, while service on the Senate Budget Committee is permanent, leading to periodic complaints that the House panel may be at a disadvantage vis-à-vis the more experienced Senate membership. But we feel the House had the right idea in exposing a broad cross section of members to the budget process. We recommend that the Senate adopt the House practice of rotation, with both chambers making the limit eight years.

Congress also needs to address the issue of joint committees.

**We believe that permanent joint committees do not usually work—the disparities in chamber size, time commitments, and outlooks make joint panels singularly ineffective—and they should be eliminated.**

To be sure, the only joint committee focused on a substantive area is the Joint Economic Committee. Joint Economic has a special history, and a unique role, and its retention would be reasonable and defensible. But we believe a stronger case can be made for eliminating it and giving its broader economic focus, including its oversight of the *Economic Report of the President*, to the two chambers' budget committees.

The other permanent joint committees exist for specific reasons. The Library and

Printing Committees act as coordinators for functions that are within the purview of the legislative branch as a whole, not the House or Senate separately. The Joint Taxation Committee is effectively a staff holding operation to serve the House Ways and Means and Senate Finance panels.

Is it really necessary to have congressional committees, with assignments and requisite responsibilities, to handle these functions? We think not. The library and printing functions, in our view, could be handled by administrative panels consisting of appropriate congressional officers, overseen by the joint leadership. The printing function itself needs a careful look: is it really appropriate for the legislative branch to have jurisdiction over most executive branch printing, via the Government Printing Office? We believe that Congress should have responsibility for congressional printing, with that responsibility handled administratively. It should transfer direct control over executive branch printing to the executive.

The Joint Tax Committee's staff is truly one of Congress' success stories, with its consistently first-rate, nonpartisan professional team. But it need not be organized as a separate congressional committee. We recommend that the Joint Tax Committee be turned into a Congressional Revenue Office, parallel to the Congressional Budget Office, or better yet, folded into CBO.

If Congress implemented these

changes, the Senate would be left with sixteen committees, and the House with seventeen (or sixteen). That would be an impressive, even staggering accomplishment— but it would not be enough. Congress should also consider committee jurisdictions, figuring out where change would be both feasible and desirable and would improve the policymaking process and its outcomes.

**JURISDICTIONAL CHANGES**

As we have emphasized, we are not advocates of a radical overhaul of committee jurisdictions, moving small and large pieces to and from all committees. We do not believe that such a change is feasible politically, and, just as important, we do not believe that it can deliver, in policy terms, what would be promised. We do, however, believe that some serious changes in committee jurisdictions should be considered, along with those that flow from the consolidation of select, joint, and narrow committees recommended above.

The tests we set are fourfold. First, jurisdictional changes should make committees more equal in breadth and workload; second, they should make substantive sense by consolidating currently divided jurisdiction in important comprehensive policy areas; third, they should identify and pull together important new policy areas; and fourth, they should not arbitrarily punish committees that have been assertive and effective and reward those that have been

*"In my [state] legislature, we only had six standing committees. Every member served on only one committee. You spent your full time on that committee. You didn't have any distractions. Each committee had basically equal power as far as jurisdictions. Although there were some more prestigious committees than others, every committee was a major committee, an 'exclusive committee,' using our terms. That problem is going to be very difficult for Congress to change, but if we ever have an opportunity to change, this is the year to do it."*

**VERBATIM FROM THE ROUNDTABLES**

slothful and ineffective.

An imbalanced committee system, in which a handful of committees are highly active and universally desirable, while others are attractive only to a narrow segment of the legislature and others consistently fail to attract a full complement of members, is unhealthy for policy and process.

It is clear that both houses suffer to some considerable degree from this problem, although the Senate did act in 1977 in ways that greatly ameliorated the situation.

**We believe it is desirable to improve the balance and attractiveness of a number of House committees, including Banking, Government Operations, Education and Labor, Judiciary, and Foreign Affairs, and to reduce to some degree the range and breadth of jurisdictions of Ways and Means and Energy and Commerce.**

But, in keeping with the fourth test mentioned above, we do not believe that the latter two committees, among the most admired and effective in Congress, should be altered dramatically without careful thought to what the consequences would be for the jurisdictions removed.

We would, however, suggest the following. Remove railroads from Energy and Commerce and shift the merchant marine part of Merchant Marine and Fisheries to consolidate transportation jurisdiction into Public Works and Transportation. Remove trade from Ways and Means and put it to-

gether with other international economic jurisdiction (including both imports and ex-
ports) in a Foreign Affairs and International
Economics Committee. Make comparable
changes in international economics in the
Senate. Consolidate jurisdiction over drugs
and narcotics control in the Judiciary Committee. Consolidate family policy in a
broadened Education and Labor Committee.
Broaden the Agriculture Committee into a
Committee on Agriculture, Nutrition, and
Hunger. Take unemployment compensation
from Ways and Means and put it in Education and Labor.

We do not pretend that these are new or
innovative suggestions; many of them were
made by the Bolling Committee and its suc-
cessor, the Patterson Committee. But they
are even more timely, and should be more
possible now.

We are frankly more vexed about what
to do with the Banking Committee. A case
can be made to dismantle it. Among the
major committees, Banking (along with
Agriculture) has been among the most
clientele oriented. Its jurisdiction over
banks could go to Energy and Commerce,
pulling together financial institutions and
markets. International financial institutions
could join international economics at Foreign Affairs. Housing might become part of
a broadened and diversified (and renamed)
Education and Labor panel.

But a case can also be made to strengthen
Banking, broadening its appeal so that it could
attract and retain more of the best lawmakers
in the House. In this case, Banking might
become the focal point for international economic policy, including trade; or it might
become the center for financial institutions,
paralleling its Senate counterpart by taking
securities from Energy and Commerce. However, the need to strengthen Foreign Affairs,
and the substantive case for putting international economics in with foreign policy, is
strong. And the long history of Banking's
accommodation to the savings and loan and
banking industries, combined with the
admirable watchdog role the Energy and Commerce Committee has played overseeing the
securities industry, make us hesitant to recommend this change. In the end, we have come
down on the side of only marginal changes in
Banking's jurisdiction, but this is clearly an
area that should be reexamined.

## COORDINATING MECHANISMS

Even if one had carte blanche to rearrange
jurisdictions as one wished, there would
be substantial overlap in broad and important policy areas, and there would be emerging issues ignored or left unidentified
by the committee system. To pull all health
jurisdiction together, for example, would
mean disrupting jurisdiction over taxation,
education, science, veterans, defense, and
other areas. However desirable it is to have
a tidy process in which only a single committee readies legislation for the floor, each
chamber must have mechanisms and strate-

gies for dealing with the fact that several committees will often demand, and merit, a piece of the action on pressing policy problems.

We have two proposals for the House in this regard, although it should be noted that they basically do not require any rules change.

> The House should make more frequent use of the ad hoc committee authority that now exists, under which the Speaker can propose to the House the creation of a temporary panel, with members drawn from a range of standing committees and a chair designated by the Speaker, to address an important policy matter comprehensively and quickly.

We would like to see the Joint Committee formally endorse the utility of the ad hoc approach, and recommend that it be used for health care reform, for example.

> The House should also stiffen multiple referral practices by regularly setting time limits and by creating the use of an amicus curiae process for referrals, in which secondary committees would not have the relevant bills directly referred to them, but would have the right to make their views known by filing "friend of the court" reports to the House floor as long  as their briefs did not delay or prevent the movement of legislation from the core committee to the floor.

For the Senate, we have similar recommendations for coping with the inevitable delays, duplication of effort, and turf wars that result when policy problems cut across jurisdictional boundaries.

> The Senate Majority Leader should be able to propose, through privileged, non-debatable motions, the creation of ad hoc committees on matters involving two or more standing committees, as well as on a few important policy matters that generate such broad interest that a single committee cannot capture the variation in opinion.

## COMMITTEE PROCESSES AND STAFF

The committee system is more than assignments and jurisdictions; it is the equivalent of the central nervous system of Congress. Every aspect of its operations should be examined and, where appropriate, changes should be made. We addressed some of those issues in our first report, including proxy voting, minority rights, and innovative information gathering. We elaborate on some of them here.

One of the real problems in Congress is that few meetings or hearings of committees and subcommittees have anywhere near the full complement of members attending. Clearly, committees have declined in stature. Instead of being regarded as a member's second most important Washington responsibility, after voting on the floor, committee meetings routinely compete, seemingly at an equal level of attention, with such other activities as constituent meetings, fund-raising, signing mail, and going to the gym. Hearings become more spectacle than substance when only the chairman is present to hear testimony, or members come in for thirty seconds to register attendance and then leave, never to return. Key debates on important issues take place with two or three lawmakers present to hear them; then votes on the amendments are decided by proxies cast for members who have no idea of what the votes were about, or of the arguments pro and con. It is no wonder that minority members, and many majority lawmakers, are frustrated with the blanket use of proxies in House committees.

As we made clear in our first report, we do not favor the elimination of proxy voting, although we do favor changes. But some methods have to be found to encourage members to show up at committee and subcommittee markups and hearings. There is no deliberative process if few show up to deliberate. Cutting assignments and thus reducing scheduling conflicts would help.

**Giving committees designated days for holding hearings and meetings, designed to minimize conflicts for those with two assignments, is highly desirable. We also strongly favor publication and widespread dissemination of committee and subcommittee attendance and voting records.**

Voting attendance matters greatly to members for floor votes—perhaps a way can be devised to make it significant politically for

committees. Congress should consider whether some type of recorded committee quorum call might be used to encourage better attendance.

It is concern over the deterioration of the deliberative process that also led us to recommend the experimentation in committees with different forms of information gathering, including seminars, roundtables, and debates.

**We also strongly favor an "early bird" requirement for each committee—questioners of witnesses called in the order in which they arrive at a hearing, not by strict seniority.**

Many committees now apply such a rule, to uniformly positive reaction.

We do not have a detailed recommendation to make about committee staffs, because there is no useful blanket reform. Some committees may be overstaffed, while others are understaffed. We do not believe generally that Congress' overstaffing is centered in the committee system. Some staff cutbacks will occur naturally as committees and subcommittees are pruned and eliminated. Large additional cuts are not necessary.

We do have one major caveat to that generalization.

**Both the House and the Senate in the past two decades have greatly expanded the committee staff available to rank-and-file members, known as "associate**

THE COMMITTEE SYSTEM 31

**staff" or, for the Senate, "S.Res. 60" or "S.Res. 4" staff. We believe these staffs should be cut back substantially or eliminated.**

As much as possible, staff resources on committees should be at the center, in the full committee and the subcommittees, available to all members but responsible primarily to chairmen and ranking members, albeit more professionalized and less patronage based. The excessive decentralization of staff resources on committees and subcommittees has contributed, in our judgment, to the difficulty committees and their leaders often have in forging consensus and moving to action. We do not want to see an era of committee dictators—as our earlier recommendation to provide the Speaker of the House the authority to declare a chairmanship vacant at any time makes clear—but we do want to see committee leaders, like party leaders, have a greater capacity, along with accountability, to set an agenda and act on it.

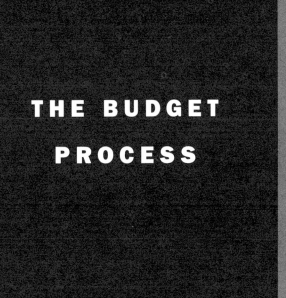

# THE BUDGET PROCESS

One important set of proposals for reforming the committee system that we have not yet considered centers on the budget process. Frustrated by the decade-long persistence of huge deficits and the complexity and duplication of the three-ring budget, authorization, and appropriations process, many critics inside and outside Congress have increasingly turned to radical proposals to simplify the process or to shift substantial powers from Congress to the president. Some advocate eliminating the budget committees and the budget resolution; others propose eliminating the appropriations committees and transferring the power of the purse to the authorizing committees; many of these same reformers are attracted to proposals like the line-item veto that circumscribe the authority of the legislative branch on budgetary matters.

We have noted a disconcerting tendency in the press to equate serious and worthy reform proposals with ones that radically restructure existing arrangements. Yet careful scrutiny often reveals the latter would very likely weaken Congress and bring on more problems than they solve. The budget process is a prime area in which students of Congress need to carefully weigh the benefits and costs of proposed reforms and, where necessary, speak forcefully against proposals that have surface popular support but might seriously harm the institution and the policymaking process.

As we make clear later, we believe it would be a mistake for Congress to eliminate a layer of the budget process—whether it be the budget resolution or the appropriations committees—or to transfer substantial budget authority to the president. But we do believe that real problems exist and that constructive changes can be implemented. We have drawn heavily on the work of our Brookings colleague Joseph White to discuss some of the problems and several possible solutions.

Congress has two stakes in the budget process. It wants a process that helps it make good policy—that produces a reasonable balance of the desires for government action, low taxes, and lower deficits. At the same time, Congress needs to ensure that its budget disputes do not paralyze Congress itself.

Since 1980 neither legislators nor the public has been satisfied with the budget process on either ground. As a result, the budget process has suffered, and Congress has suffered with it, endless revisions or "improvements." The results of those measures teach certain lessons about what might work in the future—to improve Congress' ability to deal with the deficit and to help Congress manage itself.

But we should also remember that the situation now is very different from what it was over the past twelve years. How Congress handles the budget is inextricably linked to what the president does. Many measures of the 1980s were products of competition between two branches of the government, controlled by opposite parties. The severity of many problems could be greatly diminished by more cooperation between the branches. And some of what might be done to improve the government's budget output could best be done by the executive, not Congress.

We begin by considering how the budget process shapes Congress' ability to grapple with the deficit and then assess how satisfactorily it channels the workload of Congress. At the outset we wish to make explicit our endorsement of economist Rudy Penner's now legendary formulation that "the process is not the problem, the problem is the problem." No budget process will guarantee a solution to the deficit. The 1974 Budget Act was neutral with respect to deficits; its primary objectives were to give Congress an opportunity to deal with revenue and expenditure totals and to increase the budgetary information available to it.

Yet the conflicts and statements of the past dozen years have left a legacy of unsustainable deficits. It is not unreasonable to ask whether some approaches might work better than others.

### DEFICIT REDUCTION

Four modes of deficit reduction are open to Congress.

The first mode is the normal legislative process. Annual appropriations can be cut, and authorizing committees can report legislation reducing entitlements and raising taxes, without any other processes. That is, of course, the pre-1974 system, and it worked (when it did) because of substantial presidential standard-setting through the executive budget process.

The second mode is triggered by the congressional budget process. The budget committees draft resolutions, which are debated and passed in each house; a conference version is approved; that resolution cuts the total 302(a) allocation for appropriations and instructs authorizers to report reconciliation legislation. Reconciliation is then packaged and passed. That is, in essence, the 1980-84 system. The budget resolution was in large measure used to set a standard because the president's budget was deemed unacceptable.

The third and fourth modes rely on budget summits between Congress and the president to reach agreement on some long-term deficit-reduction targets. They then create some terrible threat in hope of forcing action in one of the first two modes, as in the Gramm-Rudman-Hollings (GRH) trigger system. Or they enact the equivalent of the reconciliation legislation, determine the appropriations 302(a) in advance with a series of appropriations "caps," and create procedures that effectively prevent backing out on the deal. That is the 1990 Budget Enforcement Act (BEA) model. Each approach is a reaction to the fact that both the president's budget and the budget resolution had become efforts to avoid blame,

forcing the other branch to propose the serious measures. Only a negotiation among leaders of the two branches could produce a serious plan.

Budget reformers must begin with the lessons of these last two modes, GRH and BEA. Those rules are in place and, especially in the form of the extraordinary majorities for Senate action, have to be addressed before anything else is done.

**LEARNING FROM GRAMM-RUDMAN/ BUILDING ON BEA** In one sense, the BEA is an unqualified success. Congress and the Bush administration adhered quite closely to the constraints of "pay-go" and the appropriations caps. The process suffered fewer severe delays and upsets in 1991–92 than in most previous years. Unfortunately, the BEA, primarily owing to the intercession of a series of largely unforeseeable economic and international events and continued growth in entitlement spending, did not serve to reduce the deficit to an acceptable level.

One aspect of the BEA, a multiyear agreement between Congress and the president, is clearly useful. These agreements cannot determine most budget details—for instance, agency appropriations. But by forcing attention on long-term deficits and setting parameters for what's left of fiscal policy, these agreements provide some needed stability to budgeting. Formal efforts to mandate such a process—for example, making the budget resolution a joint resolution—risk shifting power to the president and are more likely to delay than to facilitate decisionmaking. But legislators who object to summit agreements in principle are ignoring their evident usefulness.

**We strongly recommend against Congress' devising a new deficit-reduction scheme like the old Gramm-Rudman.**

We believe President Clinton took appropriate action in retaining the flexible targets of the Budget Enforcement Act in lieu of the fixed targets of Gramm-Rudman. Fixed targets are a sham. They don't really reduce the deficit; in the five years they were tried, they were never met. That sort of approach to deficit control failed for more reasons than we can specify here, but two are particularly noteworthy. First, the hostage game, the threatened sequester of discretionary spending, could not work; hardly anyone was willing to pull that trigger. Second, since neither side wanted to specify how to meet the targets, since each dreamed the threatened sequester would force the other side to give in, and since any agreement on appropriations could be vitiated by a later sequester, there was no incentive for anyone to do anything until the very last moment.

The simple lesson is, it is much easier to design rules to prevent action, as in BEA, than to force it, as in GRH. But there are two possible elaborations.

**First, the sequester could be redesigned as something that could be allowed to happen. In other words, make the sequester a fallback position, so Congress and the president would be agreeing not on a threat but on a package of automatic deficit reductions if certain targets were not met.**

Then-Representative Leon Panetta's proposal in 1992 is an example of such an approach. Under this arrangement, Congress would adopt a standby set of deficit reductions in advance. These reductions could be across the board or distributed among programs according to the priorities established by Congress. The important thing is that they would be expressly voted on by Congress. We are not saying that those measures are politically likely, just that any set of automatic deficit reductions should be debated and adopted as if those cuts in particular will occur.

**Second, a targeting process could be designed in a way that encouraged honest proposals by the president for reducing the deficit.**

A process could set a standard for the deficit, to be triggered by a report from CBO. If CBO reported that the deficit would be too high, the president would be invited to submit a proposal to reduce the deficit by a fixed amount, say $40 billion, in the first year, with savings to be no less than that amount plus inflation and interest savings in the out years. CBO would report on the president's compliance. If he complied, that proposal would be fast-tracked through the legislative process. It would be guaranteed a vote as proposed in each chamber.

Neither of these suggestions follows the Gramm-Rudman notion of forcing congressional action. The first is itself action: the adoption of a serious backup deficit-reduction plan, to be triggered if necessary. The second admits that Congress is much more likely to act if the president leads. If Congress votes down the president's plan without replacing it, its members will get far more blame than if there is no presidential proposal at all.

Under current circumstances in the Senate, we cannot recommend eliminating the extraordinary majorities that have been built into BEA rules as a way to prevent action that would increase the deficit. If necessary, those procedures can be overridden by a presidential declaration of an emergency; if President Clinton wants to do so, he and his party should take the political credit or blame.

Neither separately nor together will the measures proposed here solve the nation's deficit problems. But all are based on a realistic appraisal of the experience of the last two decades.

**INCREASING PRESIDENTIAL POWER** Aside from modifications to the BEA-GRH structure, the major current proposals to reduce the deficit through process reform involve increasing the president's power to override Congress' decisions through measures such as a line-item veto and enhanced rescissions.

We are not quite sure why Congress would want to talk about these matters. President Clinton mentioned them in his campaign, but then most executive candidates do. These items are significant only in terms of publicity and controversy, not in their likely effect on the deficit. Even some of the most respected conservative commentators have condemned the item veto. It would clearly increase the president's power. Yet it would apply only to that part of the budget subject to annual appropriations which is growing most slowly and which can be controlled by caps. No president in the previous twelve years suggested using it for a credible amount of money. And experience in the states shows that a governor can use an item veto as a weapon in negotiating for spending he or she wants and the legislature does not; it is used more to shape priorities than to reduce spending.

An enhanced rescission is guilty of everything of which the line-item veto has been accused and more.

**But we would support an *expedited* rescission process if it were carefully designed.**

The current rescission system allows Congress simply to avoid even voting on a presidential proposal. It also allows delay that seems unnecessary. Any rescission that the president proposes is something that already passed and thus, by definition, is already familiar to the appropriations commit-tees. Rescissions ought to be guaranteed a review by the appropriators and then a re-port to the floor of the House within, say, twenty-five legislative days, with a week af-ter for the Senate. A similar process could be instituted for eliminating specific items in tax bills.

Serious issues remain on how such rescissions would be processed. Congress cannot allow the president simply to set its agenda, for instance by sending up fifty separate rescissions every two weeks, each being allowed a separate vote. Congress should also be allowed to substitute its own cuts for the president's.

> **An expedited rescission process, there-fore, must include limits on how often the president can submit rescissions (for example, three times a year) and rules about how they would be processed in committee, on the floor, and in conference. This will require careful drafting.**

**THE BUDGET RESOLUTION AND THE BUD-GET COMMITTEES** Some analysts propose to strengthen Congress for deficit reduction by strengthening the budget committees. Others argue that Congress would do better on the deficit if it abolished the entire bud-get process.

We are not sure what difference the budget process makes for deficit reduc-tion. Clearly it is not sufficient. Just as

clearly, if Congress and the president agree on both totals and details, the pro-cess is not necessary. But the latter con-dition is extremely rare.

The budget resolution at a minimum does two things.

- It provides reconciliation instruc-tions and allows committees to claim that Congress as a whole has demanded action, thus giving them cover for taking unpopular actions. Even when the process has been driven by the substantive commit-tees rather than the budget commit-tees, the former have appreciated this cover.

- It sets targets for overall spending and especially a 302(a) figure for the appropriations committees. Those committees must have some cap in order to function; they justify restraint by saying they are con-strained within an externally de-rived total. At one time they used the president's budget as their benchmark, but that became impos-sible when President Nixon and Congress sharply disagreed on both totals and priorities. One of the budget resolution's functions is to allow Congress, if it disagrees with the president, to enunciate its own targets.

It is hard to see how either of these functions could be performed without the budget resolution. But we also should be aware of what the resolution cannot do.

■ *The budget resolution cannot enforce honesty in budgeting.*

When the president fudges the numbers, Congress gets nothing but blame for being honest. Even if it does more to reduce the deficit, it can look like it does less. That is why resolutions have not in fact been more honest than presidential proposals, and why Congress gave the Office of Management and Budget the power to estimate the economy under GRH-2 and BEA.

■ *The budget resolution cannot create agreement where there is none.*

Fiscal conservatives have hoped that a vote on totals, separate from details, would provide cover for later constraint on the details of programs. In practice, Congress and the president have not allowed supposed targets from the budget resolution to interfere with the underlying process by which they set goals for totals, look at the consequences for the details, and adjust both to each other.

We believe that for deficit-reduction purposes alone there is little reason to either strengthen or abolish the budget process and committees. But there are strong reasons to alter another aspect of the process, the application of reconciliation.

One issue is the honesty of the reconciliation process. As it now operates, the process permits false or contrived savings to be substituted for real ones. It greatly overstates the amount of deficit reduction that

has been achieved and misleads Americans, especially in programs such as medicare, into fearing that valued programs are being destroyed. If Congress can demand honesty in the president's budget, it should demand no less from its own.

**Truly independent scorekeeping rules must be devised to protect Congress— and the president—against the strong temptation to cook the books.**

Another issue is whether annually appropriated programs should be subject to reconciliation. They were in 1981, but that was viewed as an egregious violation of the boundary between authorizing and appropriating. Supposedly those programs could be eliminated, if Congress wished, in the appropriations round. Since then, reconciliation has been confined to entitlements and revenues.

We believe that is a mistake. The fact is, elimination of entire programs by the appropriations committees is extremely rare. For the appropriators to abolish a government function that has been created by legislation would be a serious violation of current norms for the functions of authorizing and appropriating. If an entire agency is to be eliminated, the authorizers should do it. Put another way, which is more of a "violation" of authorizers' authority: to be ordered by reconciliation instructions to find savings, possibly including abolishing an annually appropriated program, or to have the appropriators abolish it without the authorizers having a chance to deliberate? The answer is obvious, and explains why the appropriators rarely do so.

We believe elimination or rationalization of discretionary programs, as opposed to management of routine financing needs, is legitimately a function of the authorizers.

> **Therefore, reconciliation should be extended, according to decisions in each year's budget process and by the legislative committees, to programs that are annually appropriated. When applied to discretionary authorizations, reconciliation should aim at terminating low-priority programs.**

It does not suffice to merely claim savings by lowering "authorized to be appropriated" levels somewhat below current amounts. That approach was tried in 1981, but within just a few years most of the claimed savings had evaporated.

## THE EFFECTS OF BUDGETING ON CONGRESS

In many ways the effects of the budget process within Congress are felt more personally than its effects on policy or the deficit. Its most visible parts, the appropriations and budget committees, are continually blamed for legislators' varied frustrations—though, given appropriations committees' power over matters of interest to colleagues, they are criticized far more quietly.

Many of these criticisms are misguided. Authorizations—and for that matter appropriations—have been delayed far less by the failures of, and floor time consumed by, the budget process than by the underlying policy divisions of the past twelve years. The tension between authorizers and appropriators is inherent in the two roles. If the appropriators have gained power at the authorizers' expense, that has far more to do with failures of the authorization process than with imperialism by the appropriators.

But however one allocates blame, Congress has a serious problem. For more than a decade members of most authorizing committees have felt they had little opportunity for constructive action. Since most members are not on the committees that have been active—Appropriations, the revenue committees, and, in the House, Energy and Commerce—this situation has led to immense frustration and hard feelings.

We are not persuaded that the budget process established by the 1974 Act is at the root of the problems with budgeting in Congress. It is more likely that the problems in the budget process are symptomatic of the wider difficulties Congress has had in writing authorization, appropriation, and tax bills. As such, our discussion attempts to address changes in the budget process in this wider context.

The task, as we see it, is not to punish committees—be they appropriators, fiscal policymakers, or others—but to energize the authorizing committees. To do so, we must first realize how much of their problems has been due to the budget process and how much to other factors.

## AUTHORIZERS AND BUDGETING

Legislators like to solve public problems. To do so, they often need to spend money. But for more than a decade, there has been hardly any new money to spend. At the very least, the budget process then becomes the bearer of bad news. It sets constraints that would exist anyway, but are given visible form by 302(a) allocations or reconciliation instructions.

In this situation, only two sets of committees have had elbow room. The revenue committees had it because, even if they were raising taxes or cutting spending, along the way they could provide exceptions ("transition rules") or even pay for a program expansion with a little larger cut to something they did not like anyway. Their jurisdiction is so expansive that they could find funding, at least for small favors. The appropriators had the same advantage. They had much less new money to spend than in the 1970s, but among their vast array of details and programs they had much more opportunity than other committees to do a little good for the nation or for districts here and there.

Both appropriators and the revenue committees had one other advantage: their legislation, either appropriations bills or the crucial components of reconciliation, had to pass. Even if the nation's agenda is to cut the budget, some sort of budget is still necessary.

During budget constraint, therefore, the units with most budgeting authority are far more active than all others. No process can change that: the same dynamic occurred in the executive branch as well.

But the authorizers had another, equally severe problem: divided government. It was especially serious from 1981 to 1986, when committees that wished to move legislation had to overcome not only the division between the House and the president, but in many cases extreme disagreements between the partisans who chaired the House and Senate committees.

Partisan division greatly exacerbated the budget-driven dynamic that pushed action toward the appropriations arena. A president or senator who was quite willing to torpedo an authorization could not afford to do the same with appropriations. Every one of those bills (except maybe D.C.) has something that the president, and virtually every legislator, wants. The strategic situation was exemplified on housing matters. Senator Jake Garn and the Reagan administration had no real need to settle with the House Banking Committee. But they had to deal with the Department of Housing and Urban Development/Independent Agencies Subcommittee, because that bill included the National Aeronautics and Space Administration, the National Science Foundation, and the Veterans Administration. The Banking Committee ended up having to work through the appropriators in order to preserve or alter "their" programs.

The same pattern recurred in many policy areas. Even with a united Congress, it was important when one authorizing committee had problems (for example, the foreign aid authorization). At the same time, many bills, such as the Department of Justice authorization, could involve issues that authorizing chairmen and party leaders did not want debated on the floor. It has often seemed easier to continue the programs through appropriations. The latter committees, in turn, have tried to satisfy authorizing chairmen to the extent that the latter will basically defend the appropriation on the floor; this allows appropriators to fend off accusations of a power grab and is not necessarily a bad thing for authorization chairs.

The tendency to work through appropriations has of course been exacerbated in the limited but important areas where the Senate authorizing chairman is also the Appropriations subcommittee chair. This practice should be barred.

> **Senate standing committee chairs should not be permitted to chair appropriations subcommittees, even in instances when the jurisdictions of the two panels do not coincide.**

The concentration of power is simply too much, to the detriment of both the status of Senate authorizing committees and bicameral relations with the House.

A number of these conditions (embarrassing issues, the greater likelihood of passing appropriations, and the dual roles of Senate chairmen) are not new. Neither is

tension between appropriators and authorizers. The tension is also inherently prone to differences in perception. If appropriators make concessions in conference, authorizers often believe they would not have had to—even if they would. If appropriators are asked to do ten things, do eight and add two of their own, appropriators will feel they have been very cooperative. Authorizers will blame appropriators for the two rejections and two additions; the eight agreements are simply what the appropriators should have done.

Therefore, complaints on both sides, from authorizers that they are being overrun and from appropriators that they are being importuned endlessly by ungrateful and hypocritical authorizers, are both true but not as bad as they sound. Nevertheless, the situation has been particularly bad of late, and the question is how it might be improved.

Responses may be divided into three categories: those that are occurring naturally, rules to adjust the boundary between authorizers and appropriators, and rules to improve authorizing without affecting the appropriations process.

The election of President Clinton, in and of itself, should redress much of the recent imbalance. Clinton wants to pass legislation. His agenda requires the kind of hearings and deliberation that only authorizers, not appropriators, can provide. Authorizers will have much more opportunity to act in the next four years than in the previous twelve, even as the deficit persists. The president has made clear, for example, that even as he strives to reduce the deficit, he wants to use some new revenues to fund new programs.

There have been many proposals to adjust Congress' rules and "protect" authorizers from appropriators. Almost all these proposals are in the House, where jurisdiction matters more.

> **We believe the recent proposal to give House authorizers a role in appropriations conferences involving legislation on appropriations bills is a sensible one, and we regret it was not adopted. We would like to see it given a chance.**

We do believe, however, that authorizations can be facilitated by other means. Concerns about floor time are overstated, but measures to give authorizations more time on the floor should be considered. For example, more time should be reserved early in Congress for action on authorizations, and the committees encouraged to act within that time frame. One approach would be to reverse the current understanding, which aims to move appropriations as early as possible in the House. We recognize that it would put pressure on the appropriators, but think having authorizations through the House beforehand would also help the appropriators by limiting use of the point of order against unauthorized programs.

> **Therefore, we recommend that appropriations not be allowed to come to the House floor before June 1.**

This proposal makes sense only if authorizers do, in fact, use the time provided. The Speaker's Working Group on Policy Development in the House Democratic Caucus should allocate the time and make clear to authorizers that if they do not use it, they lose it. It should also be clear that if they do not use it this year, they should not expect to get it as easily next year.

The Speaker's Working Group must also encourage authorizers to be realistic about their workloads. The 1960s and 1970s saw a move to annual authorizations. It is impossible to process that much legislation annually, and so an attempt to put pressure on appropriators with annual votes, and therefore increase authorizers' power, backfired. When authorizers could not pass their bills, they had even less claim for allegiance from appropriators (except in the special case of the Defense Department authorization, which does pass).

> **The Speaker's Working Group should accelerate the present return to multiyear authorizations by favoring committees that do so in the allocation of floor time. Congress should consider rules changes that would either ban annual authorizations or give preference to multiyear authorizations.**

These measures will not eliminate the tension between authorizers and appropriators.

But they will at least make clear that, if the appropriators are acting on programs that have not been reauthorized, this is not because the authorizers were prevented by the budget schedule from acting.

**SIMPLIFYING THE PROCESS**  Some would argue that the only way to resolve the tension between authorizers and appropriators is to abolish the latter and shift the power of the purse to the authorizing committees.  A coalition of interests, including members of authorizing committees, deficit hawks, and average citizens angered by "pork" have come to regard abolishing the appropriations committees as a panacea for problems in the budget process.  We can think of few "reforms" potentially more damaging to Congress, and less likely to succeed in achieving its purported objective, than this one.

The fact is that the appropriations committees are an essential part of Congress' division of labor, and their mode of operation and culture are starkly different from those of authorizing committees.  It is very hard to imagine that the same people could play both roles.  Having the authorizing committees perform the appropriations function would not only be difficult for them to accomplish, it would also not be very good for policy outcomes.  In the current process, the separation of authorizations from appropriations provides an extra check and balance on spending.  It is worth remembering that one major reason appropriations jurisdiction was limited

■ *"Does it make sense to authorize housing policy or urban policy every two years, so that Congress is constantly revisiting its own work as the ink is barely dry on the page? Is there anything in extending the period of time for which an authorization or an appropriation will stick, which would force Congress into looking more long range as well as short range on some of these problems?"*

**STAFF MEMBER, FROM THE ROUNDTABLES**

in the 1880s was that members of authorizing committees wanted greater control over allocating benefits through the appropriations process; the record number of freshman members who sought seats on the House Public Works and Transportation Committee in 1993 persuades us that the lessons of the 1880s are relevant to the 103d Congress. There is no reason to believe that an allocation of appropriations jurisdiction to authorizing committees would be in any way more fair or efficient than the current process, and it might well be worse.

Eliminating redundancy in the budget process is a laudable goal. But the main reason the budget process is complex is not the product of the number of committees involved but rather the fundamental complexity of the task they must perform. Eliminating the appropriations committees will not make that task any easier.

Nonetheless, we do believe it is possible to simplify the process in one important respect.

**The budget process should be performed on a two-year cycle, with basic fiscal policy guidelines set only once per Congress, in its first year.**

Biennial budget resolutions and biennial reconciliation would reduce the time devoted to budgeting and free time for other legislative and oversight activities. We are less persuaded that biennial appropriations make sense. We are not pollyannish about the impact of biennial budgeting. Setting economic projections thirty-three months as opposed to twenty-one months out will necessitate fre-

quent adjustments in the numbers, adding to the temptation to manipulate them for partisan or ideological purposes. But on balance, it would create the possibility at least of better time allocation.

Nobody should believe that process changes will eliminate the deficit. Nor should anyone imagine that internal tensions which have existed for two hundred years can be eliminated. Although we have not offered any panaceas, our proposals also are hardly business as usual. The House Appropriations Committee, for sure, will want access to the floor before June 1. The leadership may not want the responsibility for scheduling that we propose, and authorizers may object to the restrictions on annual authorizations. Forcing the president to propose honest deficit reductions is not exactly in his political interest, and declaring that any sequester Congress enacts should be one it would live with is contrary to the history of Gramm-Rudman. Expedited rescission raises many questions of power and implementation, and extending reconciliation to discretionary programs would probably meet howls of protest from both appropriators and authorizers. And biennial budgeting might well be seen as diluting the power of the budget committees.

Nevertheless, we believe all these measures are justified, and all will do some good.

# FLOOR DELIBERATION AND SCHEDULING

## SENATE

Proposing changes in the conduct of activity on the Senate floor constitutes the most difficult aspect of reforming Congress—even harder than changing committee jurisdictions—because it deals most directly with the basic nature of the institution.

While the rules of the Senate have changed very little over the past few decades, the attitudes of senators toward the institution and its processes, toward debate and toward one another, have evolved in ways that maximize the convenience of individual senators at the expense of the Senate's business. Additionally, relations between the parties have become more strained, making consensus harder to reach on Senate procedure. Rules that once served to foster debate are now used to delay legislation for frivolous reasons. Scheduling of bills on the floor—always an ad hoc, seat-of-the pants process for the Majority Leader—has become even more difficult, as the demands of fund-raising and speaking engagements keep senators from the floor. Attempts at even the most modest forms of discipline—the three-week-on, one-week-off scheduling of Senate business to ensure busy workweeks coupled with substantial time at home—quickly reverted to the Tuesday-to-Thursday-club routine.

Party leaders in the Senate are much more constrained than those in the House. Whereas the House normally plows through its legislative schedule, ignoring individual members' complaints or conflicts in favor of the conduct of the chamber's business, the Senate Majority Leader must accommodate the interests of individual senators before proceeding with the Senate's business. The Majority Leader gains nothing by attempting to bulldoze the Senate schedule or decree a plan of action, since he can be blocked by a single dissatisfied colleague. And there is always the implicit threat of opposition for reelection to his party post if the Majority Leader puts his vision of the chamber's business ahead of the care and feeding of the majority members' individual political interests and personal convenience.

Obviously, then, it is difficult for the Senate to engage reform issues that would speed up the pace of its deliberations, or introduce forcing mechanisms that limit the ability of senators to engage in extended debate. The ultimate goals of reformers also need to be clearly defined before they undertake reform. Is it to strengthen leadership, speed the pace of business, reduce the level of accommodation of individual senators, or improve the quality of debate? Some of these might require formal changes in Senate practices, while others could be implemented through leadership initiatives or the party conferences. In the House, it is easier to change discrete elements of the rules to achieve a particular reform objective. In the Senate, with less complex rules and greater reliance on unanimous consent, a seemingly modest alteration of routine can

■ *"You have to think of the Senate as if it was 100 different nations and each one had the atomic bomb and at any moment any one of you could blow up the place.  So that no matter how long you've been here or how short you've been here, you always know you have the capacity to go to the leader and threaten to blow up the entire institution.  And, naturally, he'll deal with you."*

**VERBATIM FROM THE ROUNDTABLES**

have significant effects.  Reformers must also be careful that they retain the basic nature of the Senate as a deliberative body.  We may quarrel with the quality of deliberation, but the solution is to produce processes or incentives that encourage senators to do a better job, not simply to speed up action or make the rules more efficient.  The Senate should not be reformed to look just like a smaller version of the House.

Nonetheless, change is essential.  Although the Senate likes to refer to itself as the world's greatest deliberative body, it is precisely that quality—deliberation—which is damaged by the process of endless delays and unfocused discussion that governs Senate consideration of many measures.

The Senate has become increasingly less manageable as filibusters have become virtually commonplace on both major and minor pieces of legislation, raising the standard for passage of even routine bills from fifty to sixty votes and resulting in frequent delays and uncertainties in scheduling, stop-and-go patterns of floor debate, and the use of holds and other obstructionist techniques that make the institution hostage to the whims of individual senators.

The Senate needs to create opportunities for debate to take place without the constant threat of filibuster-driven delay.

**The most significant change the Senate could consider would be to sharply restrict the use of holds for capricious**

**reasons by individual senators, and require public identification of any senator requesting a hold.**

There is no mystery why holds have become such a prominent feature of the contemporary Senate. A reliance upon unanimous consent agreements to structure debate and amending activity requires the leadership to obtain advance warning from rank-and-file senators of their intention to object to unanimous consent requests or to conduct extended debate. Increasingly, senators are subject to sophisticated demands by lobbyists to use holds on behalf of their causes; and senators have been more than willing to fully exploit the notification process on behalf of interest groups, constituents, and personal agendas. At times the practice degenerates into rolling anonymous holds as lobbyists persuade one senator after another to hold up legislation they oppose.

The real question is how—short of a major change in Rule 22—to reduce the high costs to the Senate from delays caused by objections to unanimous consent requests or by extended debate. We believe a number of changes in rules and procedures would help at the margin by contributing to greater predictability in Senate floor action.

**We start by endorsing the recommendations presented to the Joint Committee by Majority Leader George Mitchell.**

We believe that his proposals will help streamline routine aspects of Senate procedure while preserving the minority's rights

to extend debate and delay votes. He has recommended the following:

— that debate on the motion to proceed, made by the Majority Leader or his designee, be limited to two hours;

— that a ruling of the Chair in post-cloture conditions may be overturned only by sixty votes;

— that amendments reported by a committee be considered germane in a post-cloture situation;

— that time consumed on quorum calls in a post-cloture situation be counted against the senator who suggested the absence of a quorum;

— that the Senate request or agree to a conference through the adoption of a single motion, rather than three, each of which is debatable and subject to a filibuster;

— that conference reports be considered as having been read when called up for consideration; and

— that sixty senators could require that amendments to a measure be relevant.

**In addition, to further facilitate floor action, we recommend that the Senate create a committee of the whole for floor action.**

The Senate has used a committee of the whole in the past, but the mechanism was dropped in 1930 on the ground that every action it took could be repeated again outside the committee. Clearly, this objection had merit, and we do not propose reviving the committee as a mechanism to cause delay.

But we do believe that a committee of the whole, operating with more stringent debate and amendment limitations than the Senate itself, could be used to handle the bulk of less- controversial legislation, which often takes far longer to process than it needs to because senators are not used to disciplining themselves. Our proposed committee of the whole would be akin to the "Consent Calendar" process of the House for dealing with routine matters. We believe senators would welcome a process that expedited consideration of some legislation, leaving more time to devote to significant debate on controversial legislation.

In the committee of the whole the Senate would

- conduct general debate on bills, fixed by rule as in the House;

- consider legislation for amendment by title;

- allow only germane amendments;

- limit debate on amendments (to perhaps one half-hour for each side);

- limit debate on any debatable procedural motion, point of order, or appeal to thirty minutes or less; and

- further restrict debate or amendments by majority vote.

The Senate would go into the committee of the whole upon the adoption by supermajority vote of a nondebatable motion offered by the Majority Leader or his designee; the supermajority, equivalent to the vote needed to cut off a filibuster, would provide further legitimacy to the process and serve to discourage a repetition of the process outside the committee of the whole. The Senate would rise from the committee on a nondebatable motion, subject to a majority vote.

Outside the committee of the whole, the Senate would conduct its business as usual — limits on debate and amendments could be applied only by unanimous consent or by invoking cloture. In this fashion, the existing rights of senators would be preserved, and at the same time the bulk of debate on legislation would be more manageable and predictable. The Majority Leader would no longer be prevented from moving to some reasonably structured debate and amendments by individual objections to unanimous consent requests.

We also suggest that consideration be given to a number of other proposals for reducing obstructionism in the Senate.

**The Senate should require that more than one senator (perhaps three or five) object to unanimous consent requests to expedite business.**

If senators try to get around this rule by employing obstructionist quorum calls, the presiding officer should be given discretion to deny dilatory quorum-call requests and require sixty senators to overturn the ruling.

**The Senate should develop a computerized system of floor scheduling that would give all Senate offices advance notification of the Majority Leader's intention to call up listed legislation.**

Improved communication of the Majority Leader's scheduling plans may reduce the number of holds placed by senators solely for the purpose of getting timely notice from the leader. This type of hold isn't much of a problem for floor leaders, but some improvements here may reduce objections to tougher measures limiting holds.

**The Senate's party conferences should adopt formal policies on the use of holds (for example, prohibiting holds on legislation on the party's announced agenda, appropriations, and tax bills, and any legislation considered in the closing weeks of a session) and grant explicit powers to their floor leaders with respect to observing holds and maintaining the confidentiality of holds.**

The parties in this manner could empower their leaders to resist the importunings of individual senators when the interests of the party and the Senate are clearly at stake.

None of these changes, in our view, alter in any fundamental way the Senate's traditional role as a forum for the expression of minority views or as a deliberative body; indeed, having a committee of the whole might well focus general debate and provide a crispness to deliberation currently lacking in the institution.

Our final suggestion is that the Senate move to restore some integrity and meaning to the filibuster by requiring senators to engage in extended debate on the floor instead of merely issuing a threat to talk on at length.

The filibuster, as it has operated since the early 1960s, has lost its character as a classic procedure to highlight intense minority viewpoints over landmark issues. To expedite business and keep the Senate from embarrassing itself by screeching to a halt and blocking all business for a filibuster, then–Majority Leader Mike Mansfield moved to a two-track system, in which a filibuster would be announced and continue, but on an autonomous and distinct track, while other business could move forward separately.

The filibuster then evolved into a standard parliamentary weapon that simply raised the threshold on bills or nominations from fifty votes to two-thirds of those present and voting (now sixty votes). Instead of being used sparingly, for critical national issues, it became a routine process, used regularly for more mundane bills and threatened even more regularly by individual senators to gain leverage over extraneous issues.

**We recommend that the Senate return the filibuster to its classic model—if a senator declares a filibuster on an issue, he or she should be prepared for extended and continuous debate, day and night, while all other business gets put on hold.**

If senators feel strongly enough about an issue to filibuster, they should be prepared to risk ostracism from their colleagues, along with sleepless nights on narrow cots in the hallway of the Capitol.

This move does not require any rules

change; it can be implemented by declaration of the Majority Leader. We do, however, recommend an additional change that would require rules reform.

**■ We recommend that the Senate create a second class of filibuster.**

This second class would operate much as the routine, contemporary filibuster operates, on a separate track—but with two key differences. Currently, a single senator can initiate a filibuster; this Class II variety would require a petition signed by ten senators. The second difference would be about cloture petitions. As with current practice, the first cloture petition would require sixty votes to implement. But the second petition, taken at least one week after the first one, would need only fifty-five votes; the third petition, taken at least one week after the second, would require only a simple majority. If a senator wanted to bring the entire Senate to a halt, going day and night he or she could do so, and keep a high threshold of sixty votes to bring about cloture. But if the issue was not so vital, or the commitment as strong, a more limited filibuster could be initiated—with a higher standard to start it, and lower threshold to end it. Thus minority rights would be preserved, but with additional ways to expedite action.

## HOUSE

The House, unlike the Senate, has few problems disposing of legislation once it has reached the floor. The key questions involve deciding how to schedule legislation and how to ensure a deliberative process during its consideration.

As we noted in our first report, House floor scheduling has long had an ad hoc quality, dictated by the availability of bills and the wishes of committee and subcommittee chairmen. There has been little in the way of long-range scheduling over weeks and months to develop a coherent agenda for the House and to inform members what will be expected of them. Even to the degree schedules are cobbled together now, there are often last-minute changes that disrupt the plans of members and committees who schedule their work around expected floor action.

To some degree, confusion is inevitable in any legislative body, but the mechanics of scheduling too often seem to have taken control, rather than being used to support leadership policy decisions.

**■ We have recommended that the House go to a three-week-on, one-week-off scheduling system similar to the Senate's, and that floor action be intensive during the workweeks (a pattern less and less visible in the Senate). This requires a specific decision by the leadership not to accommodate the traditional Tuesday-to-Thursday-club mentality of the institution.**

We anticipate problems, and have also noted signs that the large new freshman class, in its desire to be responsive to con-

■ *"We are only here Tuesday, Wednesday, and Thursday. On Tuesdays people are flying in the morning or around noon, they check their office, they make some phone calls, they come over and vote on the Journal. On Wednesday they settle down for a day, and Thursday they have got their airplane tickets in their pockets and in the early afternoon or late afternoon they are about to leave."*

**VERBATIM FROM THE ROUNDTABLES**

stituents, would like to have frequent long weekends in their districts. But we hope members realize that their goal of ending gridlock in Congress requires them to be in Washington to do work, and that a more intelligently designed schedule will still allow them plenty of quality time at home.

We were delighted with the House majority's action last December to create a Speaker's Working Group on Policy Development. We hope that it will be given substantial responsibilities and are pleased that the group has met fairly often. However, we note that the Working Group still seems to be searching for an effective identity, and we question its larger size—thirty-eight members—which differs from the Democratic Caucus' initial decision to have a more cohesive and manageable group of twenty members.

The Working Group needs to be more than simply a debating society or a second whip meeting where members air their grievances. It should play a significant role in recommending the disposition of complicated referral questions on significant legislation and in coordinating priorities for scheduling. It can help the Speaker to use more aggressively and creatively his referral authority to set deadlines and to mesh those deadlines with decisions on advance floor scheduling.

**Suspension of the rules, which is the most frequent technique used to pass less controversial legislation, should be extended to five days a week as a scheduling tool.**

In our initial report, we speculated that the availability of this device, with proper advance notice to members and consultation with the minority, would encourage use of the early portion of a week for more substantive legislation and give members greater incentive to remain in Washington.

Perhaps the most troublesome and controversial aspect of House floor procedure results from the difficulty in striking a balance between considering legislation in a timely and orderly manner and allowing the minority party and individual members meaningful opportunities to offer alternative versions of legislation. The House debates and votes on legislation in a parliamentary situation where time is under some sort of control. It deals with an issue and moves on, in a straight line, unlike the Senate, which may never vote on a piece of legislation and shifts back and forth among pending proposals like a circus juggler. The House employs various parliamentary devices that strictly limit both the use of time and the opportunities for amendment, and others that open up the process to individual members proposing amendments or speaking. It is the balance between these devices that lets the House be representative and deliberative, but also definitive, in its actions.

The standing rules of the House provide for the one-hour rule in debate, the motion for the previous question, strict limits on the opportunity for quorum calls, strong recognition powers in the Speaker, and the ability to postpone and cluster votes, all as devices to limit delays, provide structure, and bring questions to a resolution. The minority is guaranteed in the standing rules the power to offer the motion to recommit and to control a designated share of debate time on certain measures and motions.

However, the rules are a means to an end, and the standing rules of the House do not always serve the House's interests. Special rules are required to provide for rational consideration of particular bills. The debate and amending process in the Committee of the Whole House on the State of the Union provides the most frequent opportunities for deliberation, since bills are debated and considered for amendment under the five-minute rule pursuant to a special rule reported by the Rules Committee and adopted by the House, and it is here that perceived abuses most often occur.

The minority strongly advocates the use of open rules that allow unlimited germane amendments under the five-minute rule, and has spoken sharply against the increasing use of restrictive rules. We see nothing wrong with the use of restrictive rules for managing debate, in a limited number of cases, so long as they allow sufficient deliberation on the major proposals and adequate participation by a broad range of members speaking on behalf of their constituents. There is nothing wrong with closed rules or modified rules so long as they serve these purposes.

It is impossible for the House to take the time to listen to the views of all members on all issues, nor is it desirable for members to feel they should attempt to address every issue that comes before the House. The House developed a committee system to provide for division of labor and specialization. Rules for floor consideration naturally give preference to members of the relevant committees handling a particular bill, and they should also allow access to the most vigorous opponents and those who propose significant amendments.

On the other hand, the use of these restrictive rules should not become the norm. They should be used only when necessary. An open rule should not be perceived as an aberration, a luxury the House cannot afford. The increasing practice of the Rules Committee majority of routinely announcing on the floor that a rule on a forthcoming bill might be restrictive, and providing a deadline for members to submit amendments they might wish to offer, represents a disturbing trend that should be reversed.

It is difficult to define the point at which a measure is considered under conditions unfair to the minority. Depending on the particular situation, adoption of a rule that does not permit a particular amendment to be considered could be interpreted as an attempt to silence or censure the minority; or as a management tool to save the time of the House from a frivolous amendment without significant support; or as a

policymaking device to allow the minority some access, but not so much as to let it chip away constantly at a majority proposal until it finally finds a way to weaken it. The amending process should be used by the minority as a means of sharpening its own views and drafting legislative proposals that maximize their chances of passage on the floor, not just as a means of harassing the majority or endlessly attempting to probe for weaknesses.

Problems do arise when the Rules Committee, as the vehicle for the majority to structure floor debate, goes overboard to advantage the pending legislation at the expense of alternative proposals desired by the minority or by minority blocs within the majority. These advantages can come in the form of limited debate time, limited number and disadvantageous sequence of amendments, and restrictions on the minority's right to offer a motion to recommit with instructions. The majority has developed various rationalizations for its actions—preventing excessive delays in the floor schedule, blocking harassment by the minority and floor votes intended to embarrass rather than to represent legitimate alternative views, and barring killer amendments that could gut a bill, since the minority can always vote against the bill on final passage instead. Taken together, however, they constitute a disregard for minority rights, the rights of individual members, and a dismissal of the constructive role the minority or other dissenters can play in offering alternatives and pointing out flaws in a pending measure.

> **We recommend that the minority be guaranteed the right to offer a motion to recommit with instructions, if authorized by the Minority Leader.**

The motion guarantees that the minority will always have at least one opportunity to voice its views. The majority goes too far when it tries to dictate to the minority what the minority's views might be and how they should be offered. The role of the Minority Leader should be upgraded to give the leadership responsibility for ensuring that the motion be used for purposes constructive to the minority's agenda. The Speaker should be given the power to postpone debate and votes on the motion to recommit and final passage for one legislative day, in order to encourage the majority to prepare for serious debate on the motion.

> **We also recommend that the majority allow other avenues for amendments to be offered as part of the normal amending process, and that it not approach these issues with a mind-set that the minority will get "one shot" and that this constitutes fairness.**

The bias should be toward openness unless the circumstances on a particular bill demand some sort of limitation, and even then there should be limits beyond which the majority cannot go.

## DEBATE

As we discussed in some detail in our initial report, the quality of debate in Congress has been diminished as members spend less time on the floor and come to votes preprogrammed on issues by information gleaned from staff and lobbyists. There is little real interaction and discussion among members. What passes for debate are often lonely declamations by members or senators at times when legislative business has been concluded.

> **In our first report, we recommended the use of Oxford Union–style debates as one means of encouraging deliberation on the House and Senate floor, forcing members to engage the ideas of the other party in a public setting and educating the American people on important issues facing the country.**

We are greatly encouraged by the commitment of majority leaders in both houses to proceed in this fashion. Consideration should be given to the mechanics of how these debates might be conducted and what rules are required. We favor a more formalized process in which members perform specific tasks in debate for a specified period of time.

> **What is also needed in both houses of Congress is a focus on reintegrating debate into the legislative process, rather than using it for purely individual concerns or as a form of protest, as is frequently the case in the House's special order time.**

By utilizing debate more constructively,
Congress can overcome the mind-set of
members, particularly in the House, that
debate is merely a filler time dividing periods of important activity and giving members a respite to engage in other activities.
The attitude toward general debate in the
House frequently resembles the Senate's
use of quorum calls, which are intended to
delay action while members reach the floor
or while private consultations occur.

In recent years, on some bills, notably
the defense authorization bill, the House
has broken up periods of general debate
into sections that deal with specific policy
issues in the bill. The House then considers
and votes on even more specific amendments, and might then resume debate on
some other issue. We find this practice constructive and recommend that it be used
more frequently on complex legislation, to
help members focus on broader questions as
they then move toward more particularistic
amendments. If members find that debate
can actually help them understand issues,
or is focused enough on specific policy
questions to avoid the negative perceptions
of the current process of general debate,
there will be additional incentives to come
to the floor and participate, or at least listen.

BICAMERAL
RELATIONS

Tensions between the House and Senate are a normal part of the legislative process, though there have been times when interchamber disagreements have reached proportions significant enough to endanger Congress' ability to function. Today may well be one of those times. There are a number of problems in interchamber relations that might profitably be addressed. Although it may not be possible to offer specific recommendations to change congressional practices in all cases, open discussion of them could help restore some sense of good faith among the members.

The most frequent complaints come from the House and are directed at aspects of Senate rules that delay or frustrate action on bills, that add legislative provisions which the House would rather not have considered, or that disrupt patterns of power distribution and internal negotiation in the House in conferences. While some of these complaints are amply justified, others represent the common practice of blaming differences in rules rather than focusing on more basic issues such as the inherent constitutional differences between the two chambers, or of blaming the Senate for practices also followed by the House.

Since the House is a body tightly controlled by rules designed to force it to reach conclusions on legislation, there is an inherent conflict between it and a Senate designed to slow the pace of action or prevent it altogether.

The Senate's inability to pass important legislation that could pass in the House, such as foreign aid bills, has tended to disrupt the

structure of the House committee system and the influence of individual panels. Committee work is far more significant in the House than in the Senate, and House members perceive changes in the status and power of their committees as damaging to their own reputations and influence.

The House floor schedule is geared toward consideration of measures reported from authorizing committees, but Senate inaction has helped to increase the power of appropriations subcommittees, which are called on to resolve these matters through "must pass" appropriations bills, with the authorizers placed in a subordinate negotiating role and excluded from formal participation in conferences.

In the 103d Congress, the House Democratic Caucus changed its rules to reduce the status of the Foreign Affairs Committee, which had difficulty attracting members to serve on it, in part because legislation originating there had little prospect of becoming law. Although this demotion had a great deal to do with the public's insistence in the 1992 elections on priority attention to domestic problems, there was also a latent concern that, even in a period of unified government, the Senate might still be unable to produce and secure passage of foreign policy legislation.

The Senate's loose rules on germaneness, and lax enforcement of restrictions barring substantive policy riders on appropriations bills, are the source of the greatest friction. House members view these practices as an attempt by the Senate to manipulate the legislative process to its advantage; and the House has frequently sought to restore a balance by changing its rules to allow separate House votes on issues originating in the Senate. Nevertheless, House members sometimes encourage the Senate, especially on actions which they favor but on which they would prefer to avoid casting a separate vote in the House.

The House has long had a rule that allows any member to demand a separate vote on any nongermane provision of the Senate included in a conference report. The rule was originally passed to prevent House conferees from accepting provisions the House has never voted on and would be unable to reach in a single up-or-down vote on a conference report. But there has been an increasing tendency on the part of the Rules Committee, at the behest of House conferees and the leadership, to waive this right because it might encourage further delay and threaten ultimate passage of legislation after a difficult conference negotiation.

However, going in the opposite direction in the 103d Congress, the House has moved to undermine the power of appropriations conferees to reach and promote agreements by giving the chairs of authorizing committees the right to make a preferential motion to insist on disagreement to a legislative provision. While this proposal also served the purpose of restoring some of the status lost by authorizers over the years, it potentially places obstacles in the way of votes on the conferees' recommendations and undermines the basic principle that motions related to conferences are intended to

bring the two chambers together, not perpetuate their division.

The House's objections to the presence of legislative provisions on appropriations bills must also be weighed in the context of frequent House use of the practice when it suits that body's purposes. With the help of waivers from the Rules Committee, and with the connivance of authorizing committees and the leadership, House appropriators include legislative provisions while simultaneously blaming the Senate for making the practice necessary by failing to pass authorizing bills into law.

The Senate can claim some movement toward limiting the presence of nongermane or irrelevant provisions in legislation. The Byrd rule on reconciliation, which does not exist in the House, tends to restrict the presence of items not geared toward deficit reduction. The Senate also employs supermajorities that prevent waivers of the Budget Act, a process that can be accomplished by simple majority in the House with the help of the Rules Committee.

Supermajorities are another aspect of fundamental differences between the chambers. The Senate's various sixty-vote requirements for budget act waivers, overriding certain rulings of the chair, and for other purposes, reinforce that body's emphasis on minority rights.

The House, by contrast, has almost no supermajority requirements in its rules. House members regard the Senate supermajority requirements, which sometimes manifest themselves as issues in House-Senate appropriations conferences, as holding the House hostage to Senate minorities.

Another problem in bicameral relations is the size of conference committees. The House practice of multiple referrals of legislation has led to the creation of large House delegations to bicameral conferences, with House conferees subdivided in numerous ways and often appointed with a mandate to consider a narrow range of provisions, or sometimes only a single issue. On mammoth bills such as budget reconciliation, it is impossible for all conferees to meet in the same room, and conference agreements are not so much negotiated as assembled from a massive paper flow coordinated by staff out of the numerous subconferences.

The practice has worked to the disadvantage of both bodies. The House lacks a coordinated strategy, since powerful committee chairs sometimes work at cross-purposes with one another and then require leadership intervention to negotiate seriously. This problem, Speaker Tom Foley has said, contributed to his decision to ask the House for authority to add and remove House conferees when necessary to move conferences toward resolution of disagreements. The Senate, with a small number of conferees facing a mob from the other body, is uncertain exactly with whom to negotiate and cannot tell who can deliver agreements sufficient to gather a majority of House conferees' signatures on a conference report.

Neither chamber is pure in this process. Neither chamber can amend its rules in ways that dramatically affect the status and power of the other body. Attempts to do so, such as pro-

posals that would automatically reject provisions of one chamber if it violates a rule of the other, or that require a supermajority in the House for passage of nongermane Senate amendments, can be destructive and backfire on Congress as a whole.

We are disturbed by these proposals and would urge Congress to expressly address major issues in bicameral relations, rather than allow each chamber to attempt to deal with them individually and yield potentially destructive results.

More specifically, based on our previous discussion, we recommend the following.

**Senate floor procedures should be changed in order to more strictly enforce rules regarding legislation on appropriations bills.**

**The House Speaker should reduce the size and organizational complexity of his conference appointments.**

**The House should enact an equivalent of the Byrd rule on reconciliation.**

**Joint leadership meetings should coordinate a schedule for both chambers which encourages House members and senators to remain in Washington at the same time, to ensure better communication among members and joint availability for scheduling of conferences.**

# RELATIONS BETWEEN THE PARTIES

Congress today suffers from an intense and destructive partisanship, especially in the House, that discredits the institution in the eyes of the public and diminishes the quality of life within it. This partisanship is the result of broad forces in American politics; it will not easily be cooled by structural adjustments within Congress.

Several critical developments in American politics, including the mobilization of blacks and the rise of the Republican party in the South, have contributed to an ideological consolidation within each of the parties and increasing conflict between them. This ideological sorting of the parties has reduced the incidence of cross-party coalitions in committees and on the floor, thereby diminishing opportunities for minority party members to leave an imprint on legislation.

Having served a forty-year sentence as the "permanent" minority, the longest period in American history, House Republicans have increasingly adopted a confrontational stance, seeking to highlight their differences with the Democrats and vigorously protesting the heavy-handed rule of the majority. The long period of divided government brought its own frustrations to congressional Democrats, who found their majority status of limited legislative use in the face of Republican presidents with very different agendas.

As a majoritarian institution with its rules dominated by a permanent majority party, the House was ripe for the corrosive partisanship that subsequently developed. The Senate, on the other hand, with its tradition of unlimited debate and its experience with alternating party control in the 1980s, has fewer partisan tensions. Yet even the individualistic Senate is feeling the effects of the heightened ideological conflict between the parties.

The return of unified party government may reshape the context within which this bitter partisanship flourishes, but we see no signs of deescalation in this "War of the Roses." We urged in our initial report that the House minority be given control of the motion to recommit (which we discussed earlier under floor procedure) and of one-third of the investigative staff on committees. However, developments since the election have done nothing to suggest that minority rights will win greater protection in an era of unified government. Despite the slightly increased size of the GOP minority in the House, the trend continues of restricting the minority's ability to influence floor activity and enunciate opposing views.

No significant proposals were offered in the most recent organizational meetings of the Democratic Caucus to enhance minority rights. Except for modest provisions supported by the minority dealing with oversight activities of the new bipartisan House Administration subcommittee created by last year's administrative reforms, all the movement was in the other direction. The amendments receiving the most attention were seen by the minority as attacks on its prerogatives.

The proposal for restricting time for special orders and allowing recognition for speeches only, in effect, with the permission of the leadership was intended to restrict the minority's development of special orders as a part of its agenda-setting process. It also struck at the basic representational rights of all members to speak for their constituents. The Speaker wisely retreated from this idea on the last day the Caucus met in December and created instead an informal bipartisan group to devise reforms in special orders. We hope the House moves in the direction of promoting Oxford Union–style debates on policy issues while retaining the right of individual members to express their views.

Party relations were also damaged by the proposal to allow delegates to vote in the Committee of the Whole. Although the votes of these nonmembers could be canceled out by the full House if they threatened to affect the disposition of an issue, the fact that all five were members of the Democratic Caucus fueled the minority's belief that giving a vote to the District of Columbia, the Commonwealth of Puerto Rico, and three territories was motivated not by concerns over representation and participation but by efforts to reverse the minority's ten-seat election gain. Appear-

ances were not helped by the fact that the leadership successfully put down opposition within the Democratic Caucus from members wary of the constitutional implications of the proposal.

At the committee level, the minority lost a useful tool for delaying committee action when the House is considering amendments in the Committee of the Whole. Committee chairs proposed adoption of an amendment that allows all committees to meet at any time except during joint sessions and meetings of Congress. This gave the chairs greater flexibility on scheduling committee meetings but also increased the likelihood of interruptions as members answered calls to vote on the floor.

We were also disappointed by the majority's failure to recognize the minority's legitimate claims to a fairer share of the budget for committee staffing.

**The House should adopt a rule guaranteeing the minority one-third of the investigative staff, just like the rule that now guarantees it one-third of the statutory staff.**

In a period of unified government, the minority is even more dependent on its staff for helping to develop ideas and draft legislative proposals.

We have little counsel to offer beyond the specific recommendations we have already made. A stronger, more confident House Democratic party might be persuaded to take the extra step to allow the

minority its rightful voice in the process.
A Democratic president seeking support for
his proposals on the other side of the aisle
might take the edge off partisan conflict and
encourage less confrontational tactics
among Republicans and more constructive
bargaining between the parties.  And we
hope a commitment to congressional renewal will strengthen institutional loyalties
among both Democrats and Republicans.

STAFF

*"Staff grows to meet demand. And demand [is being] driven by technology and competing special interests."*

**VERBATIM FROM THE ROUNDTABLES**

Allegations of overstaffing and ballooning congressional staff growth may be the most common contemporary complaints about Congress. Yet the primary goal of reformers should be to find ways to improve Congress' ability to perform its basic functions and institutional responsibilities as efficiently as possible. With regard to staff specifically, it follows that the goal of any reform effort should be not simply to cut staff in order to save money, or to respond to public and press criticism, but rather to allocate and use staff more effectively and to encourage professionalism so that Congress can better represent constituents and deal with the country's policy problems.

Before discussing our recommendations to reform the current system, we want to address some of the widespread misconceptions about staff and staff growth that have been repeated incessantly in recent years. Congressional staffs have grown substantially since World War II, and particularly in the past quarter-century. But nearly every account suggests that explosive growth has continued unabated through the last decade and more.

This is not true. Most staff growth occurred in the 1960s and 1970s. This growth coincided with a major reform movement that decentralized power and resources in Congress; it was also part of an overall effort to modernize the institution, to help it cope with its growing workload and establish its own independent base of information, knowledge, expertise, and analytical capability—at a time when the White House was dramatically increasing its own staff to challenge basic congressional prerogatives.

But staff growth did not continue unabated. It leveled off in the late 1970s—before the Reagan era—and has not changed materially since. Today congressional staff sizes— personal, committee, administrative, and support agency—are roughly equal to what they were ten years ago. In spite of this apparent leveling off, the calls persist for drastic, across-the-board cuts. We urge Congress not to succumb to this pressure. The more efficiently run, already overburdened, sectors of Congress would be hardest hit by such a measure. This would certainly not bring about greater institutional efficiency and would most likely increase staff turnover, which would further weaken the institution. In addition, such a cut, though it would probably reduce the overall cost of operating Congress, would make Congress more dependent on the executive branch and on interest groups for information and policy expertise. A large across-the-board cut in staff would be a penny-wise, pound-foolish approach.

The figures in table 2, taken from the new edition of *Vital Statistics on Congress*, provide a factual basis for discussing the deployment of congressional staff and the wisdom of various reform proposals.

## PERSONAL STAFF

The largest component of congressional staff consists of those employees, currently numbering 11,500, who work directly for indi-

| TABLE 2. CONGRESSIONAL STAFF, 1991 | |
|---|---|
| Staff | Number |
| Personal | 11,572 |
| ■ House | 7,278 |
| ■ Senate | 4,294 |
| Committee | 3,620 |
| ■ House | 2,321 |
| ■ Senate | 1,154 |
| ■ Joint | 145 |
| Administrative/leadership | 5,993 |
| ■ House | 1,442 |
| ■ Senate | 1,187 |
| ■ Joint | 3,364 |
| Support agency | 6,254 |
| ■ General Accounting Office | 5,054 |
| ■ Congressional Research Service | 831 |
| ■ Congressional Budget Office | 226 |
| ■ Office of Technology Assessment | 143 |
| Total | 27,439 |

vidual members of the House and Senate. House members are now authorized to hire up to eighteen full-time and four part-time or shared employees. There is no limit on the number of employees a senator may hire, but personal staff must be paid from a clerk-hire or legislative assistance allowance (the former varying by state population).

While these staff allocations to members seem more than generous, a careful study of congressional staff for the Renewing Congress Project by Lawrence Hansen (which itself will be published separately) reveals the following.

■ Although congressional staff levels have remained relatively stable for more than a decade, the workload in

personal offices has increased
markedly. The capacities of most congressional offices to process routine
work—to answer mail, reply to legislative inquires, promote federally
funded projects for their states and
districts, and service constituent requests for assistance—have reached
or are fast approaching the breaking
point. The picture that emerges is one
of desperation—of staff frantically try-
ing to keep their heads above water
and to make it through another day
in one piece.

■ Congress' growing workload (particularly in member offices) is exacting a
high cost in terms of staff morale,
burnout, and turnover. These conditions are exacerbated by four other
factors: salaries that in most cases are
uncompetitive with salaries in the
private sector; few opportunities within
congressional offices for professional
advancement; a crowded and uncon-
genial work environment; and working
hours that are uncommonly long and
very unpredictable. It is an environment that on the one hand encourages
experienced senior staff to abandon
the Hill for more lucrative private sector positions and on the other hand
appears to attract fewer young people
genuinely committed to long-term
public service.

■ A large part of Congress' burgeoning
workload is the result of extravagant
public expectations—expectations
that over the past twenty years members of Congress themselves have
consciously and sometimes foolishly
fostered. Consequently, the use of
available staff resources has also radically changed. Having flung the doors
wide open to their constituents, chiefly
for political reasons, members now
feel obliged, again because of political
imperatives, to be as responsive as
possible to all claims regardless of
their relevance or urgency. Increasingly, the public looks upon its senators and representatives not as a last
resort for relief and assistance, which
was once more commonly the case,
but as its first resort.

■ Many congressional offices add to
their workloads through mass mailings, including periodic postal patron
newsletters. Some members do not do
newsletters. And others have instituted
policies designed to minimize their
responses to the impersonal and bulk
mailings (typically postcards) they re-
ceive from constituents. Most offices,
however, attempt to respond in a
timely manner to everything that
comes through the door, creating the
illusion that citizens and their elected
officials are in close touch. The fact

*■ "One of the things somebody said to me, 'As time goes on, you will get some more staff as you get seniority.' I don't want more staff, because I'm having a hard enough time keeping up with the memos that my current staff is generating. You know, there is always so much to do, and it is the classic case of knowing how to discipline yourself, knowing what is important and what is not important, freeing yourself to think and giving yourself time to think, and also giving yourself time to be with your colleagues."*

**VERBATIM FROM THE ROUNDTABLES**

is, however, that most members read neither the incoming mail nor the outgoing replies bearing their signatures. Many staff understand the hypocrisy of the situation—and would like to find a workable and collective escape route.

There are no obvious solutions to these and related problems associated with the demand for and use of personal staffs in the House and Senate. But any steps that are taken should be geared toward the following objectives.

■ Improve the institution's capacity to recruit, retain, and develop a highly professional staff.

■ Reduce or make more manageable that portion of the congressional work load that distracts members and staff from attending more fully to their legislative and oversight responsibilities.

■ Encourage greater discipline, restraint, and accountability on the part of members and staff in the use of Congress' finite resources.

**As a first step in this direction, we recommend a reduction in the maximum allocation of full-time House employees from eighteen to fifteen, and a 5 percent reduction in each senator's clerk-hire account.**

These changes will provide some economies and encourage members to think through the allocation of their resources and responsibilities. At the same time, we believe that House office budget allotments should be left at their current level, to give members more flexibility to hire and retain professional staff members and to begin to close the gap between House and Senate staff salaries.

**In addition, existing restrictions on the ways members can allocate their office resources should be eliminated to allow members more management flexibility, but the lifting of such restrictions should be accompanied by more exacting disclosure requirements with respect to the use of such resources.**

Serious consideration should also be given to finding new ways to manage the burgeoning workload associated with casework and grass-roots campaigns and to develop more professionalized personnel and management practices in congressional offices.

## COMMITTEE STAFF

As the figures in table 2 make clear, committee staff constitute a relatively modest part of the congressional bureaucracy. Yet they are the near-exclusive focus of reformers bent on across-the-board cuts in staff. This attention is partly due to the belief in the executive branch and the private sector that committee staff have become individual power brokers who gener-

ate unnecessary work and ultimately clog the legislative process. It also reflects the unwillingness of even the most ardent critics inside Congress to entertain sizable reductions in personal staff.

We believe substantial savings can be realized here, without harming the ability of Congress to perform its constitutional responsibilities, if several principles are followed.

**Reductions and adjustments in committee staff should be made in conjunction with a consolidation and restructuring of the committee system as the number of subcommittees is reduced and as select and minor committees are merged with major committees.**

**Committee appropriations and staffing levels should be based on realistic work load projections.**

As part of this effort, and in the interest of a more rational and transparent accounting system, the distinction between statutory and investigative staff should be eliminated and a single process initiated for authorizing committee expenditures.

Finally, as we argued in our discussion of committee reform,

**associate staff positions in the House and Senate should be radically reduced or eliminated entirely.**

## ADMINISTRATIVE STAFF

A large number of congressional staff are hired to make the Capitol Hill trains run on time. The Architect of the Capitol, the Capitol Police Force, and officers of the House and Senate (such as doorkeepers, parliamentarians, sergeant-at-arms) employ legions of staff with an extraordinary range of responsibilities. Much of the hiring for these positions has been patronage based, and over the years many of the embarrassing revelations of congressional misdeeds have centered on this part of the Capitol Hill establishment.

In the last several years, Congress has begun to professionalize its administrative operations and move toward systems long in place in the executive branch and the private sector. The hiring of a Director of Non-Legislative and Financial Services in the House was a landmark in this evolution from a patronage-based to a professional administrative system. But much more remains to be done; in the process, we believe, some staff savings can be realized.

## SUPPORT AGENCIES

Congressional support agencies, the General Accounting Office, the Congressional Budget Office, the Office of Technology Assessment, and the Congressional Research Service, are an integral part of Congress and have contributed to its strength and independence, as well as to its policy and institutional knowledge and expertise. They also need to be looked at carefully.

The General Accounting Office, by far the largest support agency, has substantial audit and investigation responsibilities that go well beyond its direct work for Congress. Consequently, it is a mistake to think of GAO's 5,000 employees as all being a part of the congressional staff. But as an aggressive and resource-rich agency, it is not immune from controversy. It is probably not surprising that twelve years of divided government have made GAO a target of criticism, much of it coming from a minority party in Congress that believes the agency has been used frequently by the majority for its own purposes.

Although we do not believe that the disproportionate influence on GAO's agenda by the majority party is itself a big problem, we do feel that the process by which GAO interacts with members to establish its agenda needs rethinking. GAO is often criticized by disgruntled lawmakers for tailoring studies to individual requesters. If the agency was able to better inform all of Congress about its activities and how it sets its agenda, the perception that it is in alliance with specific members would no doubt be less.

The agency, in our judgment, has no institutional bias toward Democrats, but it does show a sensitivity toward whoever solicits its help.

**GAO needs to develop a more open process for defining problems, announcing new studies, and issuing reports.**

The problem, we want to emphasize, is not simply GAO's. Rather, Congress has not created any institutional mechanism for a regular and systematic tracking or coordination of GAO activities that can reach all its members, and the members themselves, including many who regularly criticize the agency, have shown no particular interest in finding out all that GAO is doing, and why it is doing so.

> **Committees requesting GAO studies should include ranking minority members as well as chairs in discussions with agency personnel.**

In the absence of movement in this direction, both by the agency and by Congress, we can expect more, and more bitter criticism, with a partisan edge.

Another area of controversy surrounding GAO involves the use of agency detailees by congressional committees and subcommittees. GAO assigns roughly one hundred detailees a year to committees. The majority usually end up on one of three House committees: Appropriations, Energy and Commerce, or Government Operations. In many cases these detailees are viewed as additional staff to the committee and subcommittee chairs, and therefore as putting GAO in support of the majority's agenda.

> **We recommend that Congress seriously consider eliminating concerns about partisanship, and incidentally increasing GAO's focus on auditing rather than**

> **policy prescription, by sharply reducing GAO detailees (to a maximum of fifty) and by restricting them to the process followed by the House Appropriations Surveys and Investigations staff.**

These GAO detailees are used for investigations that are approved by both the committee chair and ranking minority members, to produce studies that are not published. This approach allows Congress to use GAO's special skills without any question of partisan bias.

> **Some modest reductions in GAO staffing are possible, but Congress should proceed cautiously to avoid disrupting the agency's highly professional and productive staff.**

The three remaining agencies have generated nowhere near the controversy of GAO— in part because none have GAO's resources or power. While the Congressional Budget Office has sometimes been charged with bias, this is not generally viewed as a significant problem. CBO's greatest strength lies in its neutrality; the organization rarely makes policy recommendations and focuses instead on providing balanced analysis.

The Office of Technology Assessment is similar to CBO in its efforts to avoid taking firm stands on policy issues. The agency is considered highly credible by members of both parties and is well regarded for its technical competence. The OTA model is an interesting one. A relatively small permanent staff is supplemented by the use of outside experts on panels on a case-by-case basis.

The Congressional Research Service is probably the least controversial of the four agencies. But its role too should be considered by the Joint Committee. Its predecessor, the Legislative Reference Service, was set up in large part to act as a substitute for large personal, committee, and subcommittee staffs by providing a central core of trained professionals available to all members. The LRS was professionalized further when it was transformed into CRS, and its professional cadre was expanded and enhanced—at the same time that other staffs, in offices, in committees and subcommittees, and in other support agencies, were sharply expanded. Sorting out the functions provided by a central body like CRS from those provided by the myriad of other staff entities in Congress should be done periodically. It may be that the OTA model could be adapted in part to CRS, allowing some studies to be done in whole or in part by creating panels of outside experts, with measured reductions over time in permanent staff.

There is one other area of CRS's work that should be dealt with. The highly trained and competent professionals at CRS are not employed to carry out constituency service functions, answering inquiries from school children or voters that can and should be handled by individual members' offices. CRS's professionals should spend their time

doing the substantive work necessary to Congress' legislative functions.

In looking at the support agencies, some observers have recommended aggregate reforms. Recommendations range from consolidating some or all of the agencies' functions and streamlining congressional oversight of them, to beefing up their resources and manpower to allow them to do their jobs more effectively. We feel a better approach would be to look at each agency individually, and a more regular examination of each agency's functions for Congress, and its resources, is in order.

Nonetheless, there is one general issue concerning the support agencies that merits consideration. Under present arrangements, there are few limits on congressional offices requesting services from the support agencies. The natural attitude among members and staff is, "Why not ask for a GAO report or CRS study? All it takes is a phone call, letter, or meeting." Of course, the costs to GAO, CRS, and the public—often in the tens of thousands of dollars—are not then considered. There are no costs to members or committees associated with their requests which might promote an efficient allocation of agency resources. Free goods tend to be overused; their costs outweigh their institutional benefits.

**Congress should explore the use of vouchers, an internal accounting system, and public disclosure to reduce some of the inefficiencies inherent in the current process.**

# CONGRESS AND
# THE EXECUTIVE

The return of unified party government to Washington has raised expectations of an end to gridlock and the ushering in of an era of constructive partnership between the executive and legislative branches. There can be no doubt that divided government contributed mightily to the poisonous relations between the branches and that its disappearance removes a major obstacle to interbranch cooperation.

But it would be foolish to overlook the tension between the branches that was built into our constitutional system or to underestimate the institutional legacy of two decades of chronic conflict. The habits of assertiveness and involvement practiced in both legislative and executive settings will not be easily curbed even under unified government. And the main source of conflict—widespread disagreement over what policy choices should be made in tough budgetary times—remains very much with us.

During the period from the Civil War through the Vietnam conflict, the general thrust of change in interbranch relations involved an expanded role for the federal government, accompanied by broad congressional delegations of discretionary authority to the executive branch. Since the early 1970s, however, the opposite has been occurring. Steadily increasing reassertions of congressional authority have led to executive branch charges of "micromanagement."

These charges cannot be dismissed as mere interbranch rivalry. The effects of micromanagement by Congress are in fact real and measurable, taking the form of thousands of administrative directives, regulations, and reporting requirements written into committee reports and, increasingly, into legislation. Often Congress, so preoccupied with getting its way, overlooks the very real managerial concerns of agency administrators. Sometimes this neglect can be necessary, and even beneficial, but it can also sap agency morale, exacerbate interbranch tensions, and prevent senior officials from performing their ultimate mission of implementing policy and administering programs.

Of course, responsibility for the problems is not borne exclusively by Congress. At the direction of President Bush's White House counsel C. Boyden Gray, the executive branch on many occasions deliberately ignored or defied congressional intent, frequently exercising a kind of executive veto of legislative provisions. Gray and the White House were encouraged by the 1984 Supreme Court *Chevron* decision, which provided a loose standard giving the executive great discretion to interpret ambiguous legislative statutes; they took that discretion, in our opinion, much too far.

The Supreme Court has added to the problems of micromanagement and executive-legislative tension in other ways. The *Chadha* decision removed one of the major vehicles the legislative and executive branches used to work out their balance of responsibilities, one that gave Congress the peace of mind to extend more open-ended authority to the executive. By eliminating all legislative vetoes, the Court only encouraged Congress to find other, more subterranean vehicles with which to micromanage the regulatory process.

Executive-legislative relations should not be understood as a zero-sum game. It is in the interest of both the president and Congress to seek to strengthen each branch's comparative advantages. For the system to work at its best, Congress must deliberate about the major legislative policy options and the president must lead. Neither branch can do its own job well if it tries to do everything, without respecting the other branch's role or the limits of its own capabilities. Unified government creates opportunities for changing legislative-executive branch relations in ways that could not have occurred in an atmosphere of partisan suspicion.

Structural reforms cannot themselves provide an atmosphere of mutual respect or regular and meaningful communications between the branches. But in some areas, changes can help facilitate the process. Our goals are to provide better communication when policies are formulated and priorities set, to facilitate a climate of mutual trust so that legislative delegation and executive action can be appropriately coordinated, and to refine the definition of consultation to fit the prerogatives and goals of both branches.

To accomplish these goals, we have several suggestions.

**First, Congress needs to identify better ways to define legislative intent and to guide action.**

Making this sort of change requires self-discipline by both the president and Congress. They should reach a broad agreement that administrative regulations must flow directly from the premises of a statute, as Congress determines them, not merely from a standard, as suggested in *Chevron*, that gives undue deference to the executive's interpretation of legislative meaning. A part of that understanding should be a clearer definition by Congress of what counts as legislative intent, including the language of a statute and some additional material, such as committee reports that are explicitly approved by a committee and ratified in some fashion by Congress. Parliamentarians should work out cost-effective ways of including some legislative history explicitly in the bill approval process, so that intent can be more clearly established for the executive as well as the courts.

Obviously, when Congress can make its intent clear in the language of a statute it should, but that is not always feasible or desirable. Writing more detail into laws can mean more rigid micromanagement than leaving statutes as lean and concise as possible. We have no illusions that regularizing or codifying legislative intent in this fashion would be easy, or that it would be easy even to get both branches to agree on the criteria. The lawmaking process is unavoidably fluid and messy; it is tough enough to pass anything, much less to achieve separate votes or understandings on reports or colloquies. It requires substantial self-discipline for Congress to try to think through every exigency to build a clear-cut record of intent. Still, this period of united government provides an opportunity for key people from both the executive and legislative branches to work out new ground rules on legislative intent and administrative interpretation; the opportunity should be seized.

**Second, a system needs to be developed to coordinate executive officials' testimony to Congress.**

Over several years, top executive officials, especially cabinet officers, have spent an increasing amount of their time and energy testifying in front of an increasing array of committees and subcommittees. Congress' ability to make laws and oversee their implementation, and its responsibility to guard against executive wrongdoing, all require the presence of top executive branch officials before the legislature. But that presence should be limited to those committees and subcommittees that have official jurisdiction over the particular departments, or those where a compelling justification for requiring a Cabinet officer or other top official can be offered.

In recent years, though, a much wider range of committees and subcommittees have demanded appearances by top officials, sometimes to publicize their issues and efforts, sometimes simply for ego purposes. Each appearance by a Cabinet officer requires a substantial investment in time and staff effort by the department. The legitimate need and right of congressional panels to bring in executive officials needs to be balanced against the effi-

cient use of executive officials' time.

**We recommend that the Speaker's Working Group on Policy Development and the Senate Democratic Policy Committee act as arbiters in this process. When Cabinet and other top officials feel that an appearance is unnecessary, superfluous, repetitive, or an unwarranted strain on their resources, they should be able to appeal to the Speaker's Working Group or the Policy Committee to coordinate their testimony before committees and subcommittees.**

**Third, the Speaker's Working Group on Policy Development and the Senate Democratic Policy Committee should meet regularly with members of the Cabinet and top White House staff to exchange information on future priorities and pending action.**

The level of communications between president and Congress depends first and foremost on the willingness of the president and top congressional leaders to meet together and be open and forthcoming with one another. No structural reform can create that willingness if it does not exist. But creating a mechanism to bring top congressional and executive officials together on a regular basis can increase the possibility that each branch will be aware of what the other is doing, and decrease the possibility of clashes and misunderstanding.

Consultation between the president and Congress is a key to legislative-executive relations. Consultation, however, cannot simply mean prompt notification of an executive action, especially if it is after the fact. Consultation should mean, wherever feasible, early and frequent discussion of possible actions, and a dialogue over the pros, cons, and possible outcomes—all done before executive actions occur. These regular meetings can help; they might also obviate the need for some of the formal testimony demanded of Cabinet officials by Congress.

**Fourth, special initiatives should be taken to facilitate more productive relations between the branches in the area of national security policy.**

The end of the cold war and the return of unified party government offer a real opportunity to reduce the chronic conflict that has often characterized interbranch relations since the Vietnam War.

To begin that effort, the president must accept and publicly acknowledge a partnership between the branches in the making of foreign policy, with a legitimate role for Congress. That collaboration requires consultation with Congress before action is taken by the executive. We believe the best overall strategy is to seek to substitute early congressional involvement in the setting of broad policy goals for a reliance on detailed, restrictive, often punitive measures after the fact.

**Pursuing this strategy suggests establishing and institutionalizing a joint consulta-**

**tive group on national security policy; amending the War Powers Act by substituting an explicit consultation mechanism for the provision requiring the withdrawal of troops as a consequence of congressional inaction; encouraging presidents to seek prior congressional authorization for the use of force except in a true emergency to repel an attack; and revamping foreign assistance programs by replacing the myriad of restrictions and earmarks with a limited set of broad policy objectives.**

In addition, we support structural changes within Congress (in the committee system and the budget process) that acknowledge and give primacy to the new foreign policy issues that will increasingly occupy the attention and energy of executive branch officials.

**Fifth, we believe a move toward more multiyear budget agreements and authorizations, as discussed in our section on the budget process, would foster more productive executive-legislative relations.**

The resulting stability and accompanying reduction in year-to-year partisan and programmatic tension would allow Congress to focus on priorities other than budget wars, including oversight of existing programs.

**Finally, we urge Congress to utilize innovative forms of dialogue between the branches.**

The normal form of dialogue between executive and legislative officials is in a congressional hearing, where executive officials sit at witness tables and are questioned by lawmakers sitting on the committee dais. Opening statements are followed by fragmentary questions, done without any real continuity or dialogue as members go from one line of questioning to another in five-minute segments.

The Clinton economic summit in December 1992 showed that there are other ways to have a dialogue on important policy issues. The president has indicated that he will use that format, or variations of it, for other issue areas. Although the economic summit focused on nonelected officials, there is no reason that the format cannot be used for dialogue between legislative and executive officials. Regular meetings among members of the Speaker's Working Group, the Senate Policy Committee, and the Cabinet are one approach to interbranch communications; summits are another. We urge Congress and the White House to innovate and experiment with these and other ways to improve both communications and the deliberative process.

# CONGRESS AND THE COURTS

Judicial interpretation of statutes has become for courts an increasingly significant and time-consuming duty. Ultimately, when courts review a statute and pronounce what the legislature intended, they shape the content of the legislative work product. Although this has always been true, the impact of courts on the legislative process has become more apparent recently, when some within the judiciary have criticized Congress for the way it writes its laws and have advocated a more restrictive approach to interpreting statutes.

As Congress considers it role, several questions come to the fore. What should Congress know about the problems courts face as they seek to understand statutes? How can courts come to better understand the legislative process and legislative history? How can Congress better signal its meaning? What sort of institutional processes and mechanisms can be devised in the pursuit of these objectives? These questions have been raised and are being explored by the Governance Institute in its project on judicial-congressional relations, directed by our Brookings colleague Robert A. Katzmann. We endorse and draw heavily upon that work here.

What is at stake ultimately is the integrity of the legislative process. Insofar as courts have difficulty in understanding the legislative process that they interpret, or Congress does not provide courts with a clear sense of its meaning, then both branches have a problem in need of further attention.

Consider the following typical pattern.

Congress passes a law; the statute becomes the subject of legal action. The court must interpret the meaning of the words of the statute, but the meaning is often unclear. As the judiciary delves into the legislative history—the basis upon which judges have traditionally sought to interpret statutory meaning—the court must first determine what constitutes legislative history and how to assess its various parts, including committee reports, floor debates, and votes. The court may at times be forced to delve into layers of rules and procedures of which it has little knowledge and experience.

Sometimes the legislative history may be virtually nonexistent; in other instances, Congress may deliberately elect not to deal with difficult issues. Certainly one can point to many examples of a conscious strategy on the part of drafters to put contentious aspects of statutory meaning into committee reports as a way of obscuring controversy. However, it is also true that legislation is often ambiguous because the problems confronted cannot be easily defined and Congress lacks the expertise to resolve them. That Congress does not foresee problems arising from the statutory scheme may not always be a failure of legislative will or precision; sometimes it is too much to expect Congress to foresee all manner of developments.

It is also true that when the text of a statute is clear, resorting to legislative history may be unnecessary. But if the courts simply stick to the statutory text as a rule, even when that text is ambiguous, without an adequate understanding of the context in which legislation is considered, then arguably judges will have considerable discretion to interpret the statute, perhaps in ways Congress did not intend. It is indeed ironic that some judges and legal scholars are not averse to consulting such extratextual sources as the Federalist Papers and the records of the Constitutional Convention to better appreciate the context of the constitutional provisions that they interpret, even though they blithely deny the use of analogous materials when examining statutes.

What this means is that when Congress does not give explicit direction about its legislative intent, not only does this create added burdens for the courts, but it also increases the risk that the judiciary will interpret statutes in ways the legislature did not intend. In the absence of mutual understanding, the quality of governance will inevitably suffer.

It is, of course, too much to expect that institutions will act with perfect knowledge. Given the complexities of legislating on certain issues, it is unrealistic to believe that the legislature and the judiciary can definitively address all the problems they face. But at the very least, each can strive to overcome tensions that prevent one branch from accurately assessing the processes and outcomes of the other.

On the congressional side of the equation, the task is to find ways to make the legislative history more authoritative, and to find ways for Congress to signal its meaning more clearly and give direction about how its work should be interpreted. Clarifying statutory meaning has at least three parts. The first, relating to drafting, is in some sense preventive; that is, it seeks to anticipate potential difficulties and to deal with them before a bill becomes law. The second component focuses on the materials that constitute legal history and is geared toward finding ways for Congress to signal its meaning more clearly. The third part involves developing routinized means for the courts to transmit their opinions to Congress, identifying problems for possible legislative consideration.

**With respect to drafting, Congress should subject legislation to some central scrutiny, applying accepted standards, much like some state legislatures do.**

A checklist of common problems developed by the House and Senate legal counsels' offices should be drawn upon by members and their staffs to reduce judicial burdens and at the same time give clearer definition of legislative intent. Such a checklist, perhaps incorporated into the committee report, would focus legislators' attention on such matters as constitutional severability, civil statute of limitations, attorneys' fees, private right of action, preemption, exhaustion of administrative remedies—all issues that, when not explicitly addressed in legislation, are often left to the courts for resolution. To further improve drafting, periodic seminars involving legislative counsel and judges would be useful for members and staff alike.

**As for the second element, improving statutory clarity through legislative history, there might be ways to more sharply define the purposes and most agreed-upon background of a piece of legislation.**

As part of this effort, for example, floor managers could agree about which floor statements, colloquies, and insertions in the record should be given weight and indicate that such material, by expressed arrangement, is meant to be part of the authoritative legislative history.

**With respect to the third element, statutory revision and interbranch communication, Congress and the federal judiciary should follow the example of many states which have law revision commissions that provide for the orderly evaluation of statutes, bringing together representatives of all three branches.**

A practical example of how this might work is already under way. The Governance Institute, at the invitation of the judges of the U.S. Court of Appeals for the D.C. Circuit, and with the bipartisan support of both the House and Senate leadership, helped design a system of collecting, sorting, and circulating statutory opinions of that court relevant to congressional committees for legislative consideration. Findings indicate that in most cases Congress makes no effort to clarify legislation identified by the judiciary as having problems for interpretation, at least in part because the responsible committees are unaware of the relevant court decisions. There is also evidence to suggest that the judiciary may not know of activities on the congressional side that have bearing on the court's work. To the extent that Congress can resolve problems in statutes identified by the courts, not only will the legislature's intent be better served, but also the judicial caseload may be somewhat reduced.

The core problems of congressional-judicial relations are longstanding, and no one should have any illusions about the ease with which they can be addressed. Some issues may prove to be intractable. But the legislative branch is not without means to rise to the challenges it faces. The prospect of a Court that might seek to impose upon Congress its own rules of statutory construction could leave the legislature with little choice but to respond.

This area has little public visibility, and few members are deeply interested in it. But congressional-judicial relations are crucial to the future role and power of Congress. The Joint Committee needs to keep this subject in the forefront of its deliberations and recommendations.

# ■ CONCLUSION

This report, and the Renewing Congress Project more generally, is motivated by a belief that Congress must be strengthened, as a policymaking body and as the most crucial representative institution in our democracy. Both features of Congress have been weakened in recent years, more as a result of broad social and political forces than of developments inside the legislature.

No amount of structural change within Congress will guarantee cooperation between the branches or restore public confidence in the first branch of government. But a serious effort of self-examination and organizational renewal can help if that effort is informed by a clear view of what Congress should be, and is sensitive to the need to strike an appropriate balance between conflicting features of the institution and demands upon it.

Such an examination, we have argued, has to go back to basics—starting not by responding to public criticism but by looking at what the society and political system want and need Congress and its members to do, and then focusing on how structural change can help the legislature achieve those goals. It must look at internal procedures, and at Congress' relations with other governmental institutions and such outside forces as voters, interest groups, and the press.

The Joint Committee on the Organization of Congress is a key player in bringing about congressional renewal. But it is not the only player. The parties and leaders in both houses are themselves essential, acting through party caucuses, in other congressional committees, and on the floor. For example, campaign finance reform and ethics reform, important parts of the reform agenda, will be dealt with by a range of players inside and outside Congress. While this report is directed primarily to the deliberations of the Joint Committee, we hope that its arguments and its conclusions will reach a much larger audience in and out of Congress.

Of course, this report will not be the last word on congressional reform. Nor will it be our last word. As events and proposals move forward, the Renewing Congress Project will present additional ideas as it continues to analyze and comment on the functions and workings of our national legislature.